DALLAS COWBOYS
TRIVIA CHALLENGE

Four-time All-Pro Cornell Green picks off an interception in the end zone against the New Orleans Saints.

DALLAS COWBOYS

TRIVIA CHALLENGE

GARY W. STRATTON
and
ROBERT KRUG

TAYLOR PUBLISHING COMPANY
Dallas, Texas

Library Of Congress Cataloging-in-Publication Data

Stratton, Gary.
    The Dallas Cowboys trivia challenge.

    1. Dallas Cowboys (Football team) — Miscellanea.
I. Krug, Robert. II. Title.
GV956.D3S766   1986   796.332′64′097642812   86-5785
ISBN 0-87833-535-8

Printed in the United States of America

9 8 7 6 5 4 3 2 1

FOREWORD

t is, in a sense, a curse; an affliction none of my learned friends has been able o satisfactorily explain to me. Why is it that I'm forever scrambling to make p for forgotten anniversaries and birthdays, have a devil of a time remembering my Social Security number and couldn't tell you today's date on a bet ithout first looking at the masthead of the morning paper, but am quick as a hip on matters that have no value to anyone? Want to know the song on the ip side of The Platters' 1955 hit, "Only You"? I stand ready to bet big bucks here's not another guy on the block who can assure you it was "Bark, Battle nd Ball." Need to know the order of finish of the 1948 Olympic 100-meters? 'm your man.

I hate to brag, but you're talking to the guy who dug out the fact that equipnent manager Buck Buchanan once briefly labored as a catcher in the 3rooklyn Dodgers' organization, thus making him the only Dallas Cowboys mployee to ever also work for a major league baseball team. My boss at the ime labeled the discovery trivial. I prefer to look back on it as good, investigative reporting.

Quite honestly, I don't work at retaining such facts. It just happens. It never eally seemed important to me to know that the nickname for the Cowboys vas originally to be the Dallas Rangers or that Willie Nelson's first-ever 45 pm release came out under the name Hugh Nelson, or that Slingin' Sammy 3augh starred in an old Republic serial titled "Lone Star Ranger." So what if Roy Rogers' Christian handle was Leonard Slye and Trigger's registered name vas Golden Cloud before he was teamed with the King of the Cowboys?

There are people living in my own house who suggest from time to time that t might be more beneficial if I memorized the date on a certain wedding cerificate or got it straight that Valentine Day comes around every February omething or other.

In self defense, I have prepared an argument in my own behalf. One man's rivia, I begin with a serious look and a puff on the pipe, is another man's istory. You take V-J Day; I'll stand ready to be sure you don't miss John 3teinbeck's birthday. That you consider it vital to know when the first moon valk took place is fine. But, can you tell me when it was that Sugar Land High 3chool's Kenneth Hall raced for seven touchdowns in just the first half of play gainst Houston St. Mary's? The way I see it, we've all got our jobs to do.

Which brings me to Robert Krug and Gary Stratton, the co-authors of the ome now in your hands. Call them trivial pursuitists if you will. Personally, I iew their work as that of historians and suggest somebody give them a prize. Though I understand from reliable sources they would gladly settle for elestial sales and five-figure royalties.)

During the quarter century the Dallas Cowboys have been entertaining proessional football fans across the country, several acres of books have been lone on them. We've got biographies, autobiographies, how-to's, reflections, hoto essays, and even a few stabs at history.

I suggest to you, in all seriousness, that this book, better than any which has ppeared in the marketplace, tells the colorful, dramatic, zany, and downright un-and-games history of the Cowboys.

The only reservation I have about the book, in fact, is one born of unaashed jealousy. I wish I had beaten them to the idea.

Carlton Stowers

HOW TO ENTER THE DALLAS COWBOYS
TRIVIA CHALLENGE CONTEST

Entering the Dallas Cowboys Trivia Contest is as simple as **1, 2, 3.**

1. You must use an official entry form to submit your answers to the trivia challenge. To obtain the official entry form, send a self-addressed stamped envelope to:

> Dallas Cowboys Trivia Challenge
> Taylor Publishing Company
> P.O. Box 597
> Dallas, TX 75221-0597

2. Answer the one hundred trivia challenge contest questions throughout the book. The special contest questions are intermingled with the regular Cowboys trivia. Don't worry, they are easy to find. Here is a sample contest question:

DALLAS COWBOYS TRIVIA **1** CHALLENGE CONTEST!

An original Cowboy, this SMU graduate was the Packers' leading ground-gainer in 1957.
A. Don Meredith.   B. Don McIlhenny.   C. Keith Bobo.   D. Dave Sherer.

Remember, you must use the official entry form to enter your answers. On the back of the entry form you will find twenty-five fill-in, "Tie Breaker" questions. Fill in the answers for these questions, too.

3. Mail the completed entry with the fifty cents processing fee. All entries must be postmarked no later than November 30, 1986, and must be received no later than December 8, 1986. Entries are to be mailed to:

> Dallas Cowboys Trivia Challenge
> Taylor Publishing Company
> P.O Box 597
> Dallas, TX 75221-0597

Turn to page 198 for the official entry rules and conditions of the Dallas Cowboys Trivia Challenge Contest. *Have fun and good luck!*

CONTENTS

THE GOOD OL' DAYS   9
COACHES' CORNER   16
ROOM AT THE TOP   24
ALL IN THE FAMILY   28
GIVE IT THE OLD COLLEGE TRY   32
THE ROOKIES   44
BOWLING FOR DOLLARS   54
WHAT'S IN A NAME?   57
THE NUMBERS GAME   66
I'D RATHER SWITCH   78
DROP BACK 10 AND PUNT   84
THE ENVELOPE, PLEASE   88
YOU CAN QUOTE ME   96
TURKEY DAY   100
IT'S SHOWTIME   104
IS THERE A DOCTOR IN THE HOUSE?   110
FRIEND OR FOE   114
AUTHOR, AUTHOR   130
AGAINST ALL ODDS   138
SUPER TIMES   144
FIRST AND LAST   152
THE ONE AND ONLY   164
THE ALL-TIME TEAM   170
THE BEST MAN   171
TAKING CARE OF BUSINESS   178
JUST FOR THE FUN OF IT   184
ACKNOWLEDGEMENTS   197
DALLAS COWBOYS TRIVIA CHALLENGE
CONTEST OFFICIAL RULES   198

THE GOOD OL' DAYS

Nostalgia is "in" these days. Everybody remembers the "good ol' days." The Dallas Cowboys' association with professional football goes back even before 1960, when the team came into existence.

1 What year did the Cowboys begin their association with the Salesmanship Club game?

2 What is the oldest individual entry in the Cowboys' record book?

3 He caught three touchdown passes in a game twice in 1962.

4 He returned two interceptions for more than 50 yards in 1961.

5 An original Cowboy, he played guard his first year then moved over to become the regular center.

6 Who intercepted passes in five straight games in 1961?

7 His 30 completions in a single game in 1963 stood as a record for 20 years — and his 460 yards passing in that effort remains as the top individual mark.

Frank Clarke grabs a pass.

8 He caught touchdown passes in seven straight games (in late 1961 and early 1962).

9 He took a lateral 44 yards after a Don Bishop interception in 1963, but did not score a touchdown.

10 Who were the two players who alternated at fullback in 1963-64?

11 This offensive lineman scored a touchdown in 1968.

12 Was Bob Hayes recruited for college as a football player or for track?

13 This quarterback from South Carolina signed with the Cowboys as a free-agent running back in 1965.

14 This early-day Cowboy never missed a game while at the University of Indiana, where he played tackle and end.

15 He was the busiest ball-carrier for the Cowboys in their first pre-season.

16 This 1960 Cowboy caught 53 passes and scored 13 touchdowns in his rookie year. Who was he?

17 This 1953 third-round draft pick by Los Angeles played six years as a starting offensive lineman before joining the Cowboys.

18 Which conference were the Cowboys in during their first season?

DALLAS COWBOYS TRIVIA ① **CHALLENGE CONTEST!**

An original Cowboy, this SMU graduate was the Packers' leading ground-gainer in 1957.

A. Don Meredith. **B.** Don McIlhenny. **C.** Keith Bobo. **D.** Dave Sherer.

---

19 Which two teams did Dallas beat in the 1961 pre-season?

20 How long was the Cowboys' longest field goal in 1960?

21 What was the most number of passes the Cowboys intercepted in a game in 1960?

22 Two players had seven receptions in a game in the Cowboys' first season. Who were they?

23 What team had five fumbles against the Cowboys in the 1960 season?

24 Who was the only opponent to run back a kickoff for a touchdown against the Cowboys in Dallas' first season?

25 In 1961, he threw four interceptions — but his team beat Dallas, 31-10. Who was he?

front four players for Dallas?

29 Originally a Cleveland draft choice, he played for the College All-Stars in 1958 against Detroit, was traded to Chicago and then came to Dallas in the expansion draft.

30 He was the starting quarterback on the New York Giants' 1956 title team — years before coming to Dallas.

31 He was the oldest player on the Cowboys' first-year roster. Who was he and how old was he?

32 He was the nation's leading punter at SMU in 1957.

33 He once held the NCAA passing accuracy record, completing 61 percent of his career attempts.

34 He was the only player on an all-league (NEA) team in 1959 to be

---

DALLAS COWBOYS TRIVIA ② **CHALLENGE CONTEST!**

Who was the only Cowboy scoring three touchdowns in a game in the inaugural season?

A. Don Meredith. **B.** Don Perkins. **C.** L.G. Dupre. **D.** Gary Wisener.

---

26 This member of the New York Giants intercepted a Dallas pass and ran it back 102 yards for a touchdown in Dallas' second season.

27 Where was Eddie LeBaron practicing law when the Cowboys asked him to play for them in 1960?

28 Who were the first division champion

selected by the Cowboys in the expansion draft.

35 This Cowboy scored on a 60-yard return of a blocked field-goal attempt against the New York Giants in the final regular-season game of 1965.

36 A 1,000-yard rusher in 1959, he was Dallas' No. 2 ground-gainer behind Don Perkins in 1965.

37 Who was the first quarterback on the Cowboys' roster?

38 Where did the Cowboys hold their first training camp?

39 How tall was Eddie LeBaron?

40 What was the Cowboys' record in their inaugural season?

41 Who signed the Cowboys' Certificate of Membership as NFL commissioner?

42 What was the flagship radio station for the Cowboys in 1960-61?

43 In which baseball stadium did the Cowboys hold practice sessions in 1960?

44 Who teamed with Bud Sherman to handle play-by-play in the broadcast booth for the Cowboys in 1960?

45 From which team did the Cowboys draft Jerry Tubbs?

46 He threw four touchdown passes against Dallas in the first regular-season game.

47 The Cowboys used their first-round draft choice in 1961 in a trade — but acquired a second pick. How?

48 The Cowboys played the first game of a double header in pre-season in Cleveland in 1962. Who was the Cowboys' opponent?

49 What wide receiver who reported to training camp at St. Olaf's College was shorter than quarterback Eddie LeBaron?

50 As general manager of an NFL team before coming to the Cowboys, who did Tex Schramm hire as PR director?

Eddie LeBaron (14) had the ball first, Don Meredith (17) threw it the most and Sonny Gibbs (top), the least.

51 For what team did Tom Landry play in the NFL?

52 Which team finished below Dallas in the NFL's Eastern Conference in 1961?

53 Who were the original members of the Capitol Division in 1967?

54 National Football League teams carried 38 men on their rosters in 1960. How many did Dallas carry?

55 Why did the Cowboys schedule Friday and Saturday night games early in 1960?

56 Who was Salam Qureishi?

57 Besides flooding, what was the other hazard at Burnett Field for the Cowboys?

DALLAS COWBOYS TRIVIA **3** **CHALLENGE CONTEST!**

What year did the Cowboys move their training camp to Cal Lutheran College?

A. 1965.   **B.** 1967.   **C.** 1963.   **D.** 1969.

DALLAS COWBOYS TRIVIA ④ CHALLENGE CONTEST!

From which team did the Cowboys select L.G. Dupre in the NFL player pool?
A. Baltimore Colts. **B.** New York Giants. **C.** Cleveland Browns.
D. Pittsburgh Steelers.

58 This Cowboy was a ballboy for the team in the 1960s and '70s and later played for the club.

59 Who was the Cowboys' regular punter in 1960?

60 Who was the only quarterback selected by the Cowboys in the 1960 players pool?

61 Of the 36 players chosen by the Cowboys in the 1960 players pool, how many made the team?

62 Which teams had three players each from the players pool to make the 1960 Dallas Cowboys' roster?

63 This Pro Bowl player nearly failed to make the team after being unable to run the Landry Mile.

64 This former Syracuse defensive back played two seasons with Dallas and was named All-Pro his last year.

65 Who was the second SMU quarterback to make the Cowboys' roster?

66 His football card is No. 1 in the 1953 Bowman and 1957 Topps sets.

67 In what year did the last of the original Cowboys retire?

68 Who was the last of the original Cowboys to retire?

69 Who retired last, Don Meredith or Don Perkins?

Dallas' first All-Pro running back, Don Perkins.

70 This Cowboy came to Dallas in 196? after starting with Chicago as a defensive back and converting to offense a? San Francisco.

71 He led the league in field goals in 195? with 16.

72 Which Cowboy assistant coach started his playing career with the Boston Yanks?

DALLAS COWBOYS TRIVIA ⑤ CHALLENGE CONTEST!

Who was the first Cowboy to touch the ball in a regular season game?
A. Eddie LeBaron. **B.** Tom Franckhauser. **C.** Sam Baker. **D.** Jim Doran.

(THE GOOD OL' DAYS — ANSWERS)

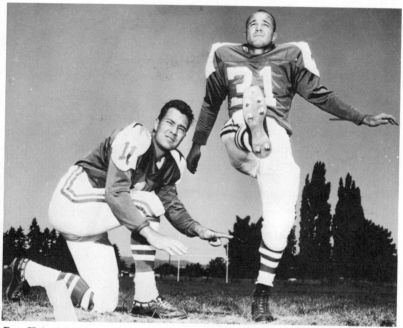

Don Heinrich (left) watches Fred Cone's field-goal attempt.

1 The Cowboys began playing the game in their first year, 1960. The game had been played 16 times before, featuring more than a dozen other teams.

2 Most passes had intercepted in a game (five by Eddie LeBaron on September 30, 1960; however, it was tied twice).

3 Frank Clarke.

4 Don Bishop.

5 Mike Connelly.

6 Don Bishop.

7 Don Meredith (he set the record against San Francisco).

8 Frank Clarke.

9 Jerry Tubbs.

10 Jim Stiger and Amos Marsh.

11 Rayfield Wright, as a tight end.

12 According to college coach Jack Gaither, football.

13 Dan Reeves.

14 Nate Borden.

15 L.G. Dupre.

16 Billy Howton with Green Bay.

17 Bob Fry.

18 Western.

19 Minnesota and Baltimore.

20 45 yards, by Fred Cone.

21 Four, against the Philadelphia Eagles in the Cowboys' second regular-season game. Dallas intercepted Norm Van Brocklin three times and Billy Barnes once.

22 Walt Kowalczyk and Jim Doran (twice).

23 The New York Giants.

24 Bobby Mitchell of Cleveland.

25 Y.A. Tittle of the New York Giants.

26 Erich Barnes.

27 In Midland, Texas.

28 George Andrie, Bob Lilly, Willie Townes, and Rocky Colvin.

29 Don Healy (a defensive tackle from Maryland).

30 Don Heinrich.

31 Fred Cone, a kicker, was 34.

32 Dave Sherer.

33 Don Meredith.

34 Duane Putman.

35 Obert Logan.

36 J.D. Smith.

Don Heinrich, a former NFL championship team starting quarterback.

37 Don Heinrich.

38 Forest Grove, Oregon.

39 LeBaron is 5 feet, 7 inches.

40 The Cowboys were 0-11-1.

41 Pete Rozelle.

42 KBOX.

43 Burnett Field.

44 Frank Glieber.

45 San Francisco.

46 Bobby Layne.

47 In a trade with the Cleveland Browns, Dallas gave up its No. 1 pick in 1961 for the Browns' No. 1 choice in 1962.

48 The Detroit Lions.

49 Cleveland Jones, who was 5 feet, 4 inches.

50 Pete Rozelle.

51 The New York Giants.

52 The Washington Redskins finished 1-12-1.

53 Dallas, Washington, Philadelphia, and New Orleans.

54 The expansion Cowboys were allowed to have a 42-man roster, but only 38 players were allowed to suit up for a game.

55 The AFL Texans had the Cotton Bowl on Sundays for the first three weeks of the Cowboys' NFL season.

56 Qureishi was assigned to develop a computer program for scouting.

57 The Cowboys also had to put up with rats at Burnett Field.

58 Mike Renfro.

59 Dave Sherer.

60 Don Heinrich.

61 Twenty-two.

62 San Francisco, Green Bay, and Los Angeles.

63 Don Perkins.

64 Jim Ridlon.

65 John Roach.

66 Eddie LeBaron.

67 1969.

68 Don Meredith.

69 Perkins retired on July 18, 1969 and Meredith on July 5, 1969. Perkins is not considered an original Cowboy because he did not play in 1960 because of an injury.

70 J.D. Smith.

71 Fred Cone.

72 Babe Dimancheff.

Jerry Tubbs made a valiant effort, but missed an opportunity to score a touchdown.

COACHES' CORNER

The Cowboys have had only one head coach in their history, but Tom Landry has had help from a couple dozen assistants during his tenure as the Cowboys' boss. Several assistants have gone on to bigger and better things . . . and some of the players have done the same.

Former Dallas assistant coaches Dan Reeves (left) and Mike Ditka. Where are they now?

1 He once returned interceptions for touchdowns in back-to-back games for the New York Giants.

2 What year did Al Lavan join the Cowboys' staff?

3 When did John Mackovic join the staff and how long was he with the Cowboys?

4 Who was Glenn Carano's Pop Warner Football League coach?

5 For which two teams was Neill Armstrong head coach before joining the Cowboys?

select as his greatest?

15 He was voted to the Pittsburgh Steelers' 50th anniversary team.

16 Which long-time American Football League coach was originally considered for the Cowboys' head-coaching job?

17 Paris had a day for him in 1979.

18 This assistant coach played for the New York Yankees and Dallas Texans. Who was he?

19 He was the NFL's All-Pro Center in 1950 and '51.

DALLAS COWBOYS TRIVIA 6 CHALLENGE CONTEST!

This one-time Cowboys receiver was an assistant coach for the Texas Wranglers in 1981.
A. Tony Hill. **B.** Percy Howard. **C.** Lance Alworth. **D.** Drew Pearson.

---

6 A former No. 1 draft choice for Philadelphia, he also spent time with the Vikings, Bears, and Oilers before joining the Cowboys.

7 This one-time assistant, and former head coach, rejoined the team in 1982.

8 Which Cowboy was coached by Amos Alonzo Stagg?

9 This Arkansas graduate was drafted by Pittsburgh, traded to Cleveland and later became a head coach, before coming to Dallas.

10 This linebacker from Oklahoma became a player-coach in 1965, in his sixth season with the Cowboys.

11 What honor did Tom Landry receive from "Football News" in 1981?

12 He was a high school quarterback in Irving before there was a Texas Stadium.

13 Which coach is credited with helping Tom Landry build the "Doomsday Defense"?

14 In the book, "Pro Football At Its Best," what game did Tom Landry

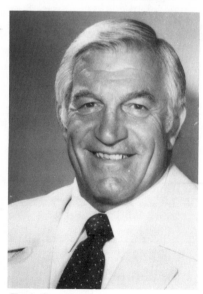

Ernie Stautner

DALLAS COWBOYS TRIVIA — 7 — CHALLENGE CONTEST!

Who was the first Cowboy coach to have a son play for Dallas?
A. Ernie Stautner.   **B.** Ray Renfro.   **C.** Tom Landry.   **D.** John Hill.

---

20 Which former assistant was a rookie tackle for the Los Angeles Rams' championship team in 1951?

21 Which assistant was a teammate of Tom Landry on the 1949 New York Yankees?

22 These three assistants joined Tom Landry's staff in 1962.

23 He played college football at both Tennessee and Duke.

24 He was the last of the original Cowboy assistants to leave.

25 Which two members of the 1964 staff also had coaching experience with San Francisco?

26 This former North Texas State standout joined Dallas in 1968 as pass-offense coach.

27 Who joined Dallas in 1968 to coach offensive ends?

28 He joined Dallas in 1968 as defensive secondary coach.

29 Who was pictured on the Cowboys' 1969 media guide?

30 When did Dan Reeves first take on coaching duties for Dallas?

31 When did Gene Stallings join the Cowboys?

32 Where did Stallings come from?

33 He came to Dallas in 1972 to assist Ermal Allen in Research and Development.

34 His home town is the same as cowboy film star Ken Maynard.

35 In March 1976, what did the City of Dallas do for the Cowboys?

36 He worked for the Cowboys in the '70s, then rejoined them as an assistant coach in '82.

37 Who was Tom Landry's head coach when he played for the Giants?

Gene Stallings

DALLAS COWBOYS TRIVIA — 8 — CHALLENGE CONTEST!

He's considered one of pro football's all-time defensive geniuses.
A. Al Ward.   **B.** Red Hickey.   **C.** Tom Landry.   **D.** Mike Ditka.

Ed Hughes

38 When did Mike Ditka join the Cowboys' coaching staff?

39 This former player caught more than 400 passes for almost 6,000 yards before becoming a Cowboys coach.

40 He coached for six other teams, including the Dallas Texans, before joining the Cowboys in 1973.

41 He played for Tom Landry from 1956 through '58 as a cornerback for the Giants and later joined the coaching staff at Dallas.

42 What year did Tom Landry retire as an active player to devote full time to coaching?

43 Who was Babe Dimancheff?

44 This Cowboy assistant was captain of his team at Purdue and made All-Midwest, All-Big Ten, and All-American.

45 Which two Cowboy coaches won more than 120 games as AFL or NFL head coaches?

46 Which coaches are still in the Cowboys' record book?

47 Before joining the Cowboys, he coached 14 years at Kentucky. He also coached under Blanton Collier and Bear Bryant.

48 Name the six teams Ed Hughes coached for before joining Dallas.

49 In addition to those six teams and the Giants, for whom he played, what other team was Ed Hughes associated with?

50 This member of the Cowboys' staff received a degree from Texas Woman's University.

51 This future Cowboy assistant was a defensive tackle for the Cowboys' first regular-season opponent in 1960.

52 What's the significance of December 28, 1959?

53 Which Dallas expansion pool pick later became an NFL head coach?

54 Who was Brad Ecklund?

55 Former 49ers head coach Red Hickey originated it in 1960. What did the Cowboys call it when they brought it back in 1974?

56 Who is the only original Cowboy player still with the team?

DALLAS COWBOYS TRIVIA **9** **CHALLENGE CONTEST!**

Who did the Cowboys defeat for Tom Landry's 200th regular-season NFL victory?

A. Washington.   **B.** New Orleans.   **C.** Philadelphia.   **D.** St. Louis.

DALLAS COWBOYS TRIVIA **10** CHALLENGE CONTEST!

What year did Tom Landry win his 100th NFL regular-season game?
A. 1971.   **B.** 1973.   **C.** 1975.   **D.** 1969.

57 This former coach grew up in the same town as Tony Dorsett and attended the same college.

58 This former player and coach caught 56 passes for 1,076 yards and scored 12 touchdowns his first year in the NFL, for another team.

59 He ranked second in longevity, as a Cowboys' assistant, to Jim Myers.

60 For which two NFL teams has Dick Nolan been head coach?

61 This former standout receiver was a coach with the Cowboys in 1985, working with the receivers.

62 He earned All-Southwest Conference honors on both offense and defense before becoming a Cowboy assistant in the 1980s.

63 Who began his head-coaching career with the Denver Gold of the United States Football League?

64 This former AFL head coach joined the Cowboys in 1973.

65 Three starters from the 1966 NFL Championship game went on to become NFL head coaches. Who were they?

66 What was the score and who was the opponent in Tom Landry's 100th win as an NFL head coach?

67 What is Tom Landry's home town?

68 Which teams did Mike Ditka play for in the NFL?

69 What was significant about Mike Ditka's first head-coaching job?

70 This Cowboy coach was born on Christmas Day.

71 Beginning in 1981, three Cowboy assistants left in consecutive years to take head-coaching jobs. Name them

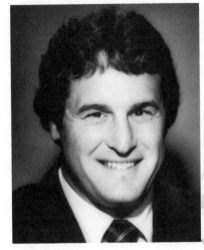

Alan Lowry

and their teams.

72 Of the three, which coach first led his team into the NFL playoffs?

73 What was the Landry Mile?

74 This two-time Cowboy later coached the San Antonio Toros of the Continental League.

75 This strength coach directed the United States weight lifting team that won the 1952 Olympics.

76 He turned down a $100,000 offer to coach Birmingham of the USFL.

77 What service did Tom Landry join during World War II?

78 What was Tom Landry's first professional team?

79 During the 1954-55 season, was Tom Landry a player or coach?

80 From which two colleges does Tom Landry hold degrees?

81 Who was the first Cowboys' assistant head coach?

82 Who is the only man who coached a professional football team for more consecutive years than Tom Landry?

83 Which two former Texas A&M head coaches went on to work as assistants with the Cowboys?

84 This former San Francisco head coach was previously a teammate of Tom Landry with the New York Giants.

85 Which former TCU head coach became a Cowboys assistant in 1983?

86 This member of the coaching staff flew B-17s over Germany.

87 Ernie Stautner picked these five Cowboys on his All-Time, All-Pro team.

88 Which future coach for the Cowboys was No. 6 in the Heisman voting in 1960?

(COACHES' CORNER — ANSWERS)

1 Tom Landry.

2 In 1980.

3 In 1981 — he coached in Dallas for two years.

4 Eddie LeBaron.

5 The Chicago Bears and Edmonton Eskimos.

6 Neill Armstrong.

7 Dick Nolan.

8 Eddie LeBaron, for one season at College of Pacific.

9 Red Hickey.

10 Jerry Tubbs.

11 Man of the Year.

12 Alan Lowry.

13 Ernie Stautner.

14 Super Bowl VI against Miami.

15 Ernie Stautner.

16 Sid Gillman.

17 Gene Stallings (and it was Paris, Texas).

18 Brad Ecklund.

19 Brad Ecklund.

20 Tom Dahms.

21 Brad Ecklund.

22 Ermal Allen, Dick Nolan, and Jim Myers.

Sid Gillman

23 Jim Myers.

24 Brad Ecklund.

25 Red Hickey and Dick Nolan.

26 Ray Renfro.

27 Raymond Berry.

28 Bobby Franklin.

29 Tom Landry.

30 In 1970, while he was still playing.

31 In 1972.

32 He had been head coach at Texas A&M before joining Dallas.

33 Sid Gillman.

34 Tom Landry.

35 Honored Tom Landry with a banquet and Tom Landry Day.

36 Alan Lowry, who worked with the Cowboys' scouting department and was an All-SWC quarterback at Texas.

37 Steve Owen.

38 In 1972, after he announced his retirement as a Cowboy player.

39 Mike Ditka.

40 Ed Hughes.

41 Ed Hughes.

42 In 1956.

43 Backfield coach on Tom Landry's staff in 1960.

44 Babe Dimancheff.

45 Tom Landry, of course, and Sid Gillman.

46 Dan Reeves, Jerry Tubbs, and Drew Pearson.

47 Ermal Allen.

48 Dallas Texans, Denver Broncos, Washington Redskins, San Francisco 49ers, Houston Oilers, and St. Louis Cardinals.

49 Los Angeles, as a player.

50 Trainer Ken Locker.

51 Ernie Stautner.

52 That was the date Tom Landry was named to coach the Dallas expansion franchise — one month before Dallas had a team.

53 Jack Patera.

54 Ecklund was one of the Cowboys' first three assistant coaches in 1960.

55 The spread formation.

56 Jerry Tubbs.

57 Mike Ditka.

58 Mike Ditka.

59 Ermal Allen.

60 San Francisco and New Orleans.

61 Drew Pearson.

62 Alan Lowry.

63 Craig Morton.

64 Sid Gillman.

65 Bart Starr, Forrest Gregg, and Dan Reeves.

66 Dallas 40, New Orleans 3.

67 Mission, Texas.

68 Chicago, Philadelphia, and Dallas.

69 He returned to Chicago, where he began his pro career.

70 Ermal Allen.

71 Dan Reeves went to Denver, Mike Ditka went to Chicago, and John Mackovic went to Kansas City.

72 Dan Reeves.

73 A distance test in Cowboys training camp. Each back was required to run the mile in less than six minutes and each lineman had to cover the course in less than seven.

74 Obert Logan.

75 Alvin Roy.

76 Gene Stallings.

77 The Air Corps.

78 The New York Yankees of the All-American Conference.

79 Both, with the New York Giants.

80 The University of Texas and Houston.

81 Jim Myers.

82 Curley Lambeau.

83 Jim Myers and Gene Stallings.

84 Dick Nolan.

85 Jim Shofner.

86 Tom Landry.

87 Mike Ditka, Bob Lilly, Chuck Howley, Forrest Gregg, and Mel Renfro.

88 Mike Ditka.

The "unemotional" coach, Tom Landry, quietly tries to make his point.

ROOM AT THE TOP

Unlike many professional sports teams, the Dallas Cowboys have been blessed with ownership stability. In fact, the Cowboys have been cast as a pattern to follow for other sports clubs — such as the Dallas Mavericks of the National Basketball Association. And the success of the Cowboys is considered by many in the organization a result of the franchise's stability.

Tex Schramm and the ultimate prize in the NFL — the championship trophy.

Q **1** Which National Football League team did Tex Schramm work for before becoming general manager of the Cowboys?

2 How did Gil Brandt make money with a camera before joining the Cowboys?

3 During the boisterous celebration by the Cowboys following Super Bowl VI, Gil Brandt was thrown into the shower. What was Brandt holding when he took his unplanned shower?

4 This Cowboy executive used to handle the substitutions for the speciality teams.

5 Who was Curt Mosher?

6 He wanted to buy the original Dallas Texans but was in South America and couldn't be contacted when the NFL told the team it had to leave Dallas.

7 How did Tex Schramm obtain information on the remaining college football talent after Dallas missed out on the 1960 draft?

Clint Murchison

DALLAS COWBOYS TRIVIA **11** **CHALLENGE CONTEST!**

Clint Murchison negotiated for three NFL teams in the 1950s before he gained an NFL franchise for expansion. Name the three teams.

A. Chicago Bears, San Francisco 49ers, Washington Redskins.
B. St. Louis Cardinals, Washington Redskins, San Francisco 49ers.
C. Baltimore Colts, Los Angeles Rams, Chicago Cardinals.
D. Chicago Cardinals, San Francisco 49ers, Washington Redskins.

---

8 What did critics call Clint Murchison's purchase of land in Irving that was to be used as a site for a future stadium?

9 Who is Bert Rose?

10 What was the address of the Cowboys' headquarters on North Central Expressway?

11 What California college awarded an honorary degree to Tex Schramm in 1977?

12 Who was named managing partner

13 What former Cowboy became an executive vice president for the Atlanta Falcons?

14 In 1968, this member of the Dallas Cowboys' staff was named chairman of the NFL rules committee.

15 Why did Clint Murchison drop his bid to buy the Washington Redskins in the 1950s?

16 What did Clint Murchison do when

when Bum Bright's group purchased the Cowboys in 1984?

Buck Buchanan — from academy to the Cowboys.

George Halas said the NFL wanted $2.5 million for a new franchise?

17 How did Clint Murchison repay Toots Shor for finding two Giants-Cowboys tickets for him?

18 Who is Larry Wansley?

19 Who are Marvin P. Knight and Pat Evans?

20 This former member of the Cowboys' executive staff was an assistant to PR director Doug Todd. He left the Cowboys for a job as PR director with the San Francisco 49ers and then went to the short-lived Philadelphia Stars of the United States Football League, where he was the general manager.

21 This Cowboy executive has become an avid fisherman and spends much of his time in the off-season chasing the blue marlin. His yacht is the Key Venture.

22 This one-time Assistant General Manager and former Public Relations director was a former sports writer.

23 What was Gil Brandt's first title with the Cowboys?

24 This former scout recommended Glen Carano to Dallas.

25 There's a stadium in the Metroplex that bears the same name as one of the Cowboys' original members of the board of directors. What is the name of the stadium?

26 Whose brainstorm idea got the dancing Dallas Cowboys Cheerleaders started toward their present style?

27 Who recommended Tex Schramm to Clint Murchison?

28 Who represented the two leagues in preliminary negotiations leading to the merger of the AFL and NFL?

29 Whose signature appears on Dallas Cowboys paychecks?

30 This former Cowboy executive went on to become a vice president with the AFC.

31 This member of the organization played football at Woodrow Wilson High School in Dallas before a knee operation forced him to change careers.

32 He joined the Cowboys in 1966 as a scout and later became Player Personnel Director.

33 He became the second member of the staff to join the team after working on the athletic staff at the Air Force Academy.

(ROOM AT THE TOP — ANSWERS)

1 The Los Angeles Rams.

2 He was a baby photographer.

3 The Lombardi Trophy.

4 Gil Brandt.

5 Mosher was the Cowboys' public relations director who went on to front-office jobs with Atlanta and St. Louis.

6 Clint Murchison.

7 Schramm paid the Los Angeles Rams $5,000 for their scouting files on players not drafted.

8 Clint's Bluff.

9 Vice president of Texas Stadium Corp.

10 6116 N. Central Expressway.

11 Cal Lutheran.

12 Tex Schramm.

13 Eddie LeBaron.

14 Tex Schramm.

15 George Marshall wanted to serve as general manager for 10 years.

16 He grabbed his chest and fell to the floor, acting as if he'd had a heart attack.

17 He sent Shor 16,000 tickets when the Giants came to the Cotton Bowl.

18 The former FBI agent hired as a security supervisor by the Cowboys.

19 Team physicians for the Cowboys.

20 George Heddleston.

21 Tex Schramm.

22 Al Ward.

23 Player scouting director.

24 Ron Meyer.

25 Amon Carter Stadium in Fort Worth.

26 Tex Schramm's.

27 Chicago Bears owner George Halas.

28 Lamar Hunt of the Chiefs for the AFL and Tex Schramm for the NFL.

29 Tex Schramm's, of course.

30 Al Ward.

31 Team physician Dr. Pat Evans.

32 Dick Mansperger.

33 Buck Buchanan.

ALL IN THE FAMILY

While many members of the Dallas Cowboys have made names for themselves, several members of the players' and coaches' families have also made noteworthy achievements.

Q

1 His wife was a member of the football pick-'em line for a Mid-Cities newspaper.

2 What did Bob Lilly's father want him to be?

3 This Cowboy's father was the first player chosen in the National Football League's 1960 draft.

4 His uncle, Ernie McMillan, played on the offensive line for the St. Louis Cardinals.

5 His brother, Doug, was the Cowboys' 14th-round draft selection in 1974.

6 This 1981 draft pick, who failed to make the cut, is the nephew of former major-league outfielder Bob Cerv.

7 Who was Glenn Carano's leading receiver during his senior year in college?

8 His brother-in-law is singer-songwriter Bill Withers.

9 His daughter is married to a former University of Texas quarterback.

10 This former Cowboy is a cousin of former Sen. Edward Brooks.

11 Randy Logan and Gregg Pruitt are his cousins.

12 His father once owned the Columbus Astros minor-league baseball team.

13 This Cowboy's wife was featured on the cover of the book, "Texas Women," a photographic study of famous and interesting women of Texas.

14 This Cowboy draft pick who failed to make the team is the brother of a former Washington Redskins defensive back.

15 He and his dad were one of only three father-son combinations both drafted in the first round of the NFL draft.

16 He and his father, also a quarterback in college, are both in the Arizona State Sports Hall of Fame. Name them.

17 His father was an All-Pro receiver for Cleveland.

18 This 1985 draft pick was born in Scotland and his father was at one time a guard at Buckingham Palace.

19 What former Cowboys player was married to actress Joey Heatherton?

DALLAS COWBOYS TRIVIA **12** **CHALLENGE CONTEST!**

A city park was named after his father, Ray, in his home town.

A. Roger Staubach.   **B.** Tom Landry.   **C.** Billy Cannon.   **D.** Billy Parks.

Glenn Carano, the Cowboys' twin quarterback.

20 His wife is an accomplished vocalist and frequently performs at Dallas Mavericks home games.

21 Their wives were co-owners of "In-Look Hair Designs."

22 When did Roger Staubach meet his future wife?

23 His brother Pumpsie was a major league baseball player.

24 This All-American had two brothers who played football at the University of Texas (Austin).

25 This late-round (No. 12 in 1973) draft choice of the Cowboys came into the league after his brother, an All-American at Arizona, was already a linebacker for the St. Louis Cardinals.

26 His younger brother was an All-American center at UCLA.

27 This Cowboy pick's brother played for the rival Washington Redskins and had annual verbal wars with Cowboys quarterback Roger Staubach.

28 This Cowboy superstar married the daughter of the Harlem Globetrotters' Marques Haynes.

29 His father was a member of two Mexican World Cup soccer teams.

30 He was one of 14 children and explained his name by saying it was either that or numbers.

31 This Cowboy's taller brother (by about five inches) was a member of an NCAA championship team and a key member of a National Basketball Association championship team.

32 Name three members of the Silver Season squad whose fathers played in the NFL.

33 Roger Staubach's father played semi-pro in two sports. What were they?

(ALL IN THE FAMILY — ANSWERS)

A

1 Larry Cole's wife, Linda.

2 A quarterback.

3 Billy Cannon Jr.

4 Howard Richards.

5 Golden Richards.

6 Derrie Nelson.

7 His twin brother, Gene.

8 Butch Johnson.

9 Tom Landry. Daughter Kitty married Eddie Phillips.

10 Butch Johnson.

11 Beasley Reece.

12 Robert Steele.

13 Charlie Waters' wife, Rosie.

14 Tim Lavender, brother of Joe Lavender.

15 Billy Cannon Jr., (and his father Billy Cannon). The other combinations were Dub and Bert Jones and Ed and Brad Budde.

16 Danny White and his father, Whizzer.

17 Mike Renfro. His father is Ray Renfro.

18 Crawford Ker.

19 Lance Rentzel.

20 Rafael Septien.

21 Benny Barnes' wife, Joyce, and Robert Newhouse's wife, Nancy.

22 In grade school.

23 Cornell Green.

24 Don Talbert.

25 Jim Arneson.

26 Bruce Walton.

27 Don Talbert, whose brother Diron Talbert played for the 'Skins.

28 Drew Pearson.

29 Rafael Septien.

30 D.D. Lewis.

31 Bruce Walton.

32 Danny White, Billy Cannon Jr., and Mike Renfro.

33 Baseball and football.

ONE IF BY LAND

A check of the list of Dallas Cowboys 100-yard rushing days shows Tony Dorsett with the best effort (206 yards) ... as well as the second best, third best, etc., etc. Dorsett has nine of the top 10 single-game efforts on the books, but he's not alone.

Ten Cowboys have run for 100 or more yards in a single game. Here's a list of the 10, and their best individual efforts:

Tony Dorsett	206 yards vs. Philadelphia, Dec. 4, 1977 (23 carries).
Calvin Hill	153 yards vs. San Francisco, Nov. 10, 1974 (32).
Duane Thomas	*143 yards vs. San Francisco, Jan. 3, 1971 (27).
Don Perkins	137 yards vs. St. Louis, Oct. 28, 1962 (24).
Robert Newhouse	124 yards at St. Louis, Dec. 16, 1973 (19).
Scott Laidlaw	122 yards vs. Washington, Nov. 23, 1978 (16).
Walt Garrison	121 yards vs. Washington, Dec. 9, 1972 (10).
Amos Marsh	117 yards vs. Cleveland, Dec. 2, 1962 (17).
Dan Reeves	114 yards at Cleveland, Sept. 17, 1967 (18).
Preston Pearson	101 yards vs. Green Bay, Oct. 19, 1975 (15).

* — Playoff game.

Mike Renfro's touchdown reception came years after many catches by his dad, also an NFL receiver.

GIVE IT THE OLD COLLEGE TRY

Where would the National Football League be without the college football teams? Texas, Oklahoma, USC, and the rest all provide the pros with their players. And, of course, the Cowboys have found a few prospects in some far away places like Fort Valley State, Ouachita Baptist, Langston, and Elizabeth City State.

Q

1 What two Heisman trophy winners played for the Cowboys at the same time?

2 How many Midshipmen have played for Dallas?

3 Where did Ed (Too Tall) Jones play college football?

4 Where did defensive back Ed Jones play college football?

5 What college did Craig Morton attend?

6 He was Iowa's heavyweight weight lifting champion in the mid-1960s.

7 Where did Roger Staubach attend school before he entered the Naval Academy?

8 While scouting for the Dallas Cowboys, Bucko Kilroy once timed a Florida player in the 40-yard dash inside an unusual building. What was it?

9 He was a teammate and played the same position as Ray Perkins at Alabama.

10 This future Cowboy was one of the few blacks given a scholarship to

Tony Dorsett

New York's exclusive prep school Riverdale Country School.

11 What was Richmond Flower athletic specialty in college?

12 He backed up Joe Theismann in college before joining the Cowboys.

DALLAS COWBOYS TRIVIA **13** CHALLENGE CONTEST!

He was a record-setting passer at Sunset High School in Dallas.

A. Jerry Rhome. **B.** Don Meredith. **C.** Drew Pearson. **D.** Don Heinrich.

13 Tony Dorsett rushed for 303 yards in a college game. Name the opponent.

14 In how many games (regular season) did Tony Dorsett run for 100 or more yards during his senior year at Pitt?

15 This player, who joined Dallas in a trade, didn't win a Heisman but did play quarterback at Boston College.

16 In the early 1970s, four Boston College exes were associated with the Cowboys. Name them.

17 He was a teammate of major-league baseball player Mike Epstein in college.

18 He played two years at Brigham Young before transferring to Hawaii.

19 What else did the Cowboys' first three draft picks from Hawaii have in common?

20 This Rice back was involved in one of college football's most bizarre, controversial plays and is known more for that play than any other. He came to Dallas in a trade with Pittsburgh.

21 This defensive back played on the same college team as Gale Sayers.

22 He was named the outstanding high school player in Texas during his senior year and was the NCAA's leading passer during his senior year.

23 He was the first college runner to carry the ball more than 1,000 times during his collegiate career.

24 His first major college appearance was in a 41-7 loss to Penn State, when he threw two passes, one an interception.

25 Who was the Cowboys' running back from Kutztown State?

26 Who was the offensive lineman from Fort Valley State?

27 Who was the All-Pro offensive lineman from Virginia Union?

28 These two Cowboys from Hawaii were on hand for the team's third trip to the Super Bowl.

29 Who was the defensive back from Morgan State?

30 Who was Grady Hurst?

31 As a quarterback, he led his college team to 32 victories in 36 games in the early 1970s.

32 Even before he was signed by the Cowboys, this player earned $150,000 for an endorsement.

33 Who was Jack Gaither's favorite athlete?

DALLAS COWBOYS TRIVIA **14** CHALLENGE CONTEST!

He was the Big Ten's Most Valuable Player in 1977.

A. Tom Randall. **B.** Jim Jensen. **C.** Larry Bethea. **D.** Robert Shaw.

DALLAS COWBOYS TRIVIA **15** CHALLENGE CONTEST!

Who was the first Cowboy draftee from Baylor University?

A. L.G. Dupre. **B.** E.J. Holub. **C.** Bobby Crenshaw. **D.** Sonny Davis.

34 Who finished higher in the Heisman voting, Randy White or Danny White?

35 Don Meredith finished in the top 10 Heisman voting twice. Name the years and where he finished.

36 What do the Cowboys entitle their annual "recruiting" mailout to college seniors?

37 Have the Cowboys ever signed any Dallas college players other than those who attended SMU?

38 Why did Roger Staubach spend one year at another school before entering the Naval Academy?

39 With which Big Ten school did Roger Staubach originally sign?

40 What were Texas and Navy ranked before Roger Staubach's Cotton Bowl game following the 1963 season?

41 Was Roger Staubach a regular or future draft pick with the American Football League?

42 Who were the opposing quarterbacks when Navy played Cal in 1964?

43 Other than being Heisman trophy winners from Navy, what else did Roger Staubach and Joe Bellino have in common during the 1960s?

44 Six future Cowboys were on the roster when the College All-Stars played Cleveland in 1965. Name them.

45 Roger Staubach's 21 pass completions against Texas in the Cotton Bowl was a record. But how did Staubach fare as a rusher?

Roger Staubach — without the star.

46 What college did Ron East attend?

47 This former San Jose State quarterback was cut by the Cowboys — but returned to California to play for the 49ers.

48 Which college did Dan Reeves attend?

49 Which other Cowboy offensive lineman attended the same school in the 1970s?

50 Has Dallas ever had a player from Austin Peay on the roster?

51 This sixth-round 1964 draft pick was a quarterback at Georgia Tech ... but was the punter for the Cowboys that fall.

52 He was the second North Texas State ex to play for Dallas.

53 Preston Pearson was the second Dallas running back from Illinois. Who was the first?

54 He was the first player from Villanova to join the Cowboys.

55 Dallas had 15 draft choices in 1962

L.G. Dupre

and five of them were from the Southwest Conference. Name the five from the SWC.

56 Which other college had two draft picks by Dallas in 1962?

57 He rushed for almost 3,000 yards in college despite being injured in a near-fatal auto wreck prior to his junior year.

58 He played no college football but was captain of the Tennessee basketball team and an All-Southeastern Conference pick.

59 He was the Gulf South Defensive Player of the Year as a junior.

60 Who was the other first-round draft choice in 1974, besides Ed (Too Tall) Jones?

61 Where did Keith Bobo go to college?

62 He led the nation in scoring his senior season at UCLA.

63 He led the NAIA in total offense with 3,167 passing yards and 251 rushing yards in his senior season (1973).

64 Wilbert Montgomery was his college teammate at Abilene Christian University.

65 Who was the Cowboys' first All-American from Arizona State?

66 He was Mississippi State's Most Valuable Player in 1975.

67 In 1953, his 493 rushing yards was a record at Baylor.

68 What college did Don Heinrich attend?

69 This original Cowboy attended Rice and was once the second-ranked all-time Green Bay receiver.

70 He came to Dallas as a free agent from Oregon State and was expected to try out at end. He later played fullback. Name him.

71 He was ranked in the NCAA's top 10 in receiving as both a junior and senior before joining the Cowboys in 1977.

72 He was a three-year starter at tackle in college (at Temple), but has played guard, center, and tackle for Dallas.

73 He hoped to make it as a back after being drafted in 1978, but was told he'd have to play tight end. He never made it with the Cowboys but starred at tight end later in his career.

74 He was the second University of Houston running back to play for the Cowboys.

75 Who was the first linebacker ever drafted by the Cowboys?

76 Who was the first kicking specialist ever drafted by Dallas?

	16	
DALLAS COWBOYS TRIVIA		CHALLENGE CONTEST!

Who was named the Outstanding Offensive Player in the 1977 Cotton Bowl?

A. Alois Blackwell. **B.** Joe Montana. **C.** Phil Pozderac. **D.** Todd Christensen.

77 He was the Southwest Conference's No. 2 rusher behind Earl Campbell during his senior year at Houston.

78 What position did Thomas (Hollywood) Henderson play in college?

79 He helped his team win the NAIA national championship in 1972.

80 He led the nation in interception yardage in 1976 at USC.

81 Who was Dallas' second draft pick from Nevada-Las Vegas?

82 Who was the first?

83 He caught 120 career passes for Santa Clara in the late 1970s.

84 In 1978 and '79, Dallas had a total of three draft picks from Southern Cal. Who were they?

85 How many times was Dennis Thurman an All-American?

86 How many career interceptions did Dennis Thurman have in college?

87 Who was the 1976 Junior College Player of the Year?

88 He led the nation in pass completions in 1958 at Baylor.

Ed Jones

Dennis Thurman on his toes.

89 Which future Cowboy, and former Texas schoolboy, quarterbacked the 1959 College All-Stars?

90 He was one of the leading ground gainers at Oregon State — but did as little running as possible for the Cowboys.

91 This former backfield mate of Jim Brown at Syracuse came to Dallas in a trade in 1963.

92 He was the Wyoming High School Player of the Year during his senior year — and remained in his home state for his collegiate career.

93 Name the five Pacific 10 players the Cowboys drafted in 1983.

94 Who was the Cowboys' "Big Game Hunter" from Salem?

95 This service academy quarterback signed a contract with Dallas, but unlike Roger Staubach never made the club.

96 He started 40 straight games at tackle for Missouri before being drafted by the Cowboys.

97 Who was the Cowboys' second draft choice from Missouri in 1981?

98 He led the nation in receiving as a college senior in 1975.

99 These two Cowboys were teammates at South Carolina State for three years.

100 This draft pick was the No. 4 scorer in the nation — and the 10th-ranked punter — at Georgia Tech in the early 1960s.

101 He was a passer and kicker from Cincinnati in 1965, but the Cowboys drafted him as a safety in the seventh round.

102 This 1965 draft selection from Auburn was named to the 1963 Associated Press and "Look" All-America teams.

103 This No. 1 draftee was Dallas' second No. 1 pick of the 1970s to play college football in the State of Tennessee.

104 Who was the first?

105 Who was the first Kentucky State player ever taken in the first round of the college draft?

106 Who are the only Fighting Irish to ever play for the Cowboys?

107 What world record were Mike Gaechter and Mel Renfro a part of?

108 During his senior year at Washington, he once threw 137 passes without an interception.

109 This 1984 draft pick was Montana's all-time leading receiver.

110 Which two defensive linemen from Arizona State spent 1982 on the injured-reserve list?

111 This future running back was an outside linebacker in high school until his junior year.

112 Whose record did Tony Dorsett break in becoming college football's all-time leading rusher?

113 He once wore a Superman costume for a magazine picture in college.

114 This former high school all-state quarterback switched positions in college and graduated from Stanford at age 20.

115 He was a city Punt, Pass and Kick champion in Mesa, Arizona.

116 This one-time Cowboy quarterback was one of the NCAA's leading passers in both 1950 and '52.

117 Which college did Bob Hayes attend?

118 As a backup running back in college in 1961, this future Cowboy averaged more than 10 yards per carry.

119 He was the first Kangaroo to play for the Cowboys.

120 He played his college football at Texas Western (before the school became UT-El Paso).

DALLAS COWBOYS TRIVIA **17** CHALLENGE CONTEST!

This offensive tackle was the first of the Cowboys' non-collegians.

A. Bob Lilly.   **B.** George Andrie.   **C.** John Gonzaga.   **D.** Rayfield Wright.

121 The Cowboys' other Hayes came to Dallas in 1963 from Humbolt State. Who was he?

122 Why wasn't Don Heinrich among the nation's top college passers in 1951?

123 This defensive tackle played high school and college ball in Lubbock.

124 He was an All-American quarterback at SMU as both a junior and a senior.

125 He was the first Razorback to play for Dallas.

126 He played fullback and center, in addition to linebacker, at Oklahoma.

127 He completed more than 69 percent of his pass attempts as a sophomore collegian.

128 This two-time All-Southwest Conference performer was moved from receiver to linebacker with the Cowboys in 1961.

129 He gained national attention his senior year at Mississippi by kicking a controversial, last-second field goal to beat Arkansas, 10-7.

130 Which Paris, Texas native was an All-Southwest Conference football and basketball player at SMU?

131 Who was the former Oklahoma quarterback who played in the Cowboys' secondary in 1961?

132 Which three colleges had three players on the Cowboys' first-year roster?

133 Who was the "best linebacker" Bear Bryant ever coached?

Mike Clark

134 Where did Jerry Rhome finish his collegiate career?

135 He was the first Cowboy ever signed out of Trinity.

136 In his senior year, he passed for 32 touchdowns and had just four interceptions.

137 He was the first Texas Aggie to play for the Cowboys.

138 Who was the first Oklahoma State Cowboy to join the Cowboys?

139 Who was the second Texas A&M grad to play for Dallas?

140 He was an NCAA punting champion at Tennessee.

DALLAS COWBOYS TRIVIA **18** CHALLENGE CONTEST!

This Cowboy tackle went to college at Heidelberg.

A. Jim Boecke.　**B.** Bob Lilly.　**C.** Rayfield Wright.　**D.** Jim Ray Smith.

141 In between the Air Force Academy and Hawaii, where did Larry Cole go to college (for one semester)?

142 Rival coach Bear Bryant called him the best SEC linebacker since Lee Roy Jordan.

143 What was Lance Alworth's position at Arkansas?

144 He was a college teammate of Mercury Morris.

145 This former offensive tackle played at Southern Mississippi and Abilene Christian.

146 He was the first Louisiana State ex to play for the Cowboys.

147 He once held the NCAA record for most receiving yards in a game (203) playing for Iowa State against Oklahoma in 1949.

148 He was the all-time ground-gaining leader at Penn before playing safety for the Cowboys.

Tex Schramm (left) looks on as Glynn Gregory signs a contract with the Cowboys; Gregory's family backs him up.

(GIVE IT THE OLD COLLEGE TRY — ANSWERS)

1 Roger Staubach and Tony Dorsett.

2 One — Roger Staubach.

3 Tennessee State.

4 Rutgers.

5 The University of California.

6 John Niland.

7 New Mexico Military Institute.

8 The Jacksonville (Florida) Airport terminal.

9 Dennis Homan.

10 Calvin Hill.

11 The hurdles.

12 Bob Belden.

13 Notre Dame.

14 Eleven.

15 Jack Concannon.

16 Bill Thomas, John Fitzgerald, Jack Concannon, and assistant coach Ernie Stautner.

17 Craig Morton (at the University of California).

18 Golden Richards.

19 All three started their college careers elsewhere before transferring to Hawaii.

20 Dick Maegle, who set a Cotton Bowl rushing record, was the star in the 1954 Cotton Bowl. He was tackled by Alabama's Tommy Lewis, who came off the bench as Maegle was streaking down the sideline. Referees awarded Maegle the touchdown.

21 Mike Johnson.

22 Jerry Rhome.

23 Tony Dorsett.

24 Roger Staubach.

25 Doug Dennison.

26 Rayfield Wright.

27 Herb Scott.

28 Larry Cole and Golden Richards.

29 Mark Washington.

30 The quarterback Danny Whi replaced at Arizona State.

31 Danny White.

32 Tony Dorsett.

33 Bob Hayes. Hayes was coached Gaither at Florida A&M.

34 Each finished ninth — Danny 1973 and Randy in 1974.

35 In 1958 he finished ninth and 1959 he finished third.

36 "Life With The Dallas Cowboys."

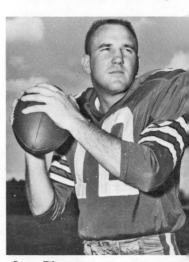

Jerry Rhome

37 Yes, Ike Thomas of Bishop College in 1971.

38 He failed English when he took the exam for the Naval Academy.

39 Purdue.

40 Texas was ranked No. 1 and Navy No. 2.

41 A 15th round future pick.

42 Roger Staubach and Craig Morton.

43 Each had his college jersey number retired.

44 Roger Staubach, Lance Rentzel, Ralph Neely, Malcolm Walker, Craig Morton, and Bob Hayes.

45 Staubach rushed 12 times, losing 47 yards.

46 Montana State.

47 Steve DeBerg.

48 South Carolina.

49 Jay Saldi.

50 Yes, Percy Howard.

51 Billy Lothridge.

Calvin Hill

52 Beesley Reece.

53 Cyril Pinder (he was on the roster in 1973).

54 John Babinecz.

55 Sonny Gibbs and Bobby Plummer of TCU, Robert Moses of Texas, Guy Reese of SMU, and Robert Johnston from Rice.

56 Southern Illinois: John Longmeyer and Amos Bullocks.

57 Robert Newhouse.

58 Larry Robinson. He played running back for Dallas in 1973.

59 Ken Hutcherson.

60 Charles Young.

61 SMU.

62 Efren Herrera.

63 Clint Longley.

64 Clint Longley.

65 Bob Breunig.

66 Jim Eidson.

67 L.G. Dupre.

68 Washington University.

69 Billy Howton.

70 Amos Marsh.

71 Tony Hill.

72 Jim Cooper.

73 Todd Christensen.

74 Alois Blackwell.

75 E.J. Holub.

76 Harold Deters in 1967.

77 Alois Blackwell.

78 Defensive end.

79 Harvey Martin (from East Texas State).

80 Dennis Thurman.

81 Aaron Mitchell.

82 Glenn Carano.

83 Doug Cosbie.

84 Dennis Thurman in 1978, and Tim Lavender and Garry Cobb in 1979.

85 Twice.

86 Thirteen.

87 Ron Springs.

88 Buddy Humphrey.

89 Buddy Humphrey.

90 Kicker Sam Baker.

91 Jim Ridlon.

92 Jim Eliopulos (a 1982 draft choice).

93 Jim Jeffcoat, Mike Walter, Bryan Caldwell, Chris Schultz, and Al Gross.

94 Monty Hunter.

95 Leamon Hall of Army.

96 Howard Richards.

97 Ron Fellows.

98 Butch Johnson.

99 Dextor Clinkscale and Angelo King.

100 Billy Lothridge.

101 Brig Owens.

102 Jimmy Sidle.

103 Robert Shaw.

104 Ed (Too Tall) Jones of Tennessee State.

105 Rod Hill.

106 Bob Belden and Phil Pozderac.

107 They were members of an Oregon relay team that set a 440-yard world record.

108 Steve Pelluer.

109 Brian Salonen.

110 Bryan Caldwell and Mike Langston.

111 Tony Dorsett.

112 Archie Griffin's.

113 Tony Dorsett.

114 Tony Hill.

115 Danny White.

116 Don Heinrich of Washington.

117 Florida A&M.

118 Bob Hayes.

119 Gene Babb. He was from Austi College, whose nickname i Kangaroos.

120 Wayne Hansen.

121 Wendell Hayes.

122 He was sidelined with a shoulde injury.

123 Bill Herchman.

124 Don Meredith.

125 Jim Mooty of Arkansas.

S stands for Steve, as in Pelluer.

26 Jerry Tubbs.

27 Don Meredith.

28 Sonny Davis of Baylor.

29 Allen Green.

30 Glynn Gregory.

31 Jimmy Harris.

32 Baylor, SMU, and College of the Pacific.

33 Lee Roy Jordan.

34 Tulsa.

35 Obert Logan.

36 Jerry Rhome.

137 Kicker Mike Clark.

138 Walt Garrison.

139 Bobby Joe Conrad.

140 Ron Widby.

141 The University of Houston.

142 Steve Kiner of Tennessee.

143 Tailback.

144 Duane Thomas.

145 Byron Bradfute.

146 Billy Truax.

147 James Doran.

148 Fred Doelling.

A guide for prospective Cowboy rookies.

THE ROOKIES

It's always been an uphill battle for first-year players to make it in the National Football League and it's especially tough to make it with the Dallas Cowboys as a rookie. But every year, new players step in and contribute. The most impressive rookie crop grew up in 1975 — and earned its own nickname.

Q

1 What was the nickname given to the 12 first-year players who helped Dallas to a 10-4 regular-season record and a trip to Super Bowl X?

2 Most rookie quarterbacks are confined to carrying a clipboard. But Gary Hogeboom played in two games his first year. What was the occasion?

3 Who was the first Cowboy to be named to the "Pro Football Digest" All-Rookie team?

4 Which Cowboy — and which future Cowboy — were named to the All-Rookie team in 1977?

5 Did Danny White make the All-Rookie team?

6 This rookie scored on two 45-yard touchdown receptions in his first two regular-season games with the Cowboys.

7 What two players from the Dirty Dozen became regulars in their first year?

John Niland

DALLAS COWBOYS TRIVIA **19** CHALLENGE CONTEST!

In only his fourth game as a Cowboy, Bob Hayes scored on two touchdown catches. Who threw the passes?

A. Don Meredith and Eddie LeBaron. **B.** Craig Morton and Don Meredith.
C. Roger Staubach and Craig Morton. **D.** Craig Morton and Jerry Rhome.

---

8 Of the Dallas Cowboys' 18 draft choices in 1975, how many made the team?

9 These two players weren't rookies but

they were newcomers, along with the Dirty Dozen, on the 1975 Dallas roster.

10 Which two schools provided two

players each to the Dirty Dozen?

11 He turned out to be the most successful of the former World Football League players on the Dallas Cowboys' 1976 roster.

12 This rookie free agent caught 22 passes during the 1973 regular season and added four more — including a pair of touchdowns — during the playoffs.

13 How old was Jean Fugett when he reported to the Cowboys?

14 He started every game as a rookie in 1973.

15 He led the team in sacks as a rookie in 1973 with nine.

16 Did No. 1 draft choice Bill Thomas ever lead the Cowboys in rushing?

17 In his rookie season (1974), he scored once every four times he carried the ball.

18 He was used primarily on passing downs the first half of 1974 but still made most of the all-rookie teams.

19 As a rookie, he tied the NFL record with a 98-yard punt return.

20 Tom Landry decided he could play any one of the four defensive line positions if he failed to make it at middle linebacker.

21 Who set the record for most punt returns in 1976 as a rookie?

DALLAS COWBOYS TRIVIA **20** **CHALLENGE CONTEST!**

He was the Cowboys' last draft pick in 1973 but played two years as a running back (only four of the other 16 draft picks played longer).

A. Les Strayhorn. **B.** Rodrigo Barnes. **C.** James Ford. **D.** Dan Werner.

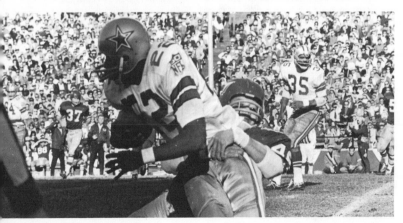

Bob Hayes on another gainer.

22 Who was the only rookie free agent to make the team in 1976?

23 He led the team in punting in 1976, his rookie year, with the third worst average in club history.

24 Was anyone drafted ahead of Tony Dorsett in 1976?

25 He set the club record for touchdowns rushing (12) in his first season.

26 When did Tony Dorsett get his first starting assignment?

27 Who backed up Bob Breunig at middle linebacker in 1977?

28 Who finished second on the team to Harvey Martin in quarterback traps in 1979?

29 His NFL debut resulted in one completion in six attempts and just six yards in a 48-7 loss to Cleveland.

30 He gave the Cowboys' special teams a new look in 1964, his rookie year, with more than 30 returns.

31 He was the first Cowboy to rank in the league's top 10 in kickoff returns as a rookie.

32 He made two runs of more than 75 yards in his rookie year. Who was he — and who were the victims?

33 Who was the oldest "Super Bowl

34 He was a ball boy in training camp as a teen-ager and then signed as a free agent in 1980.

35 He led the Los Angeles Rams in interceptions in his rookie year (1950)

with 12 before playing with the Cowboys 10 years later.

36 He was the first "future" draft pick to make it with Dallas.

37 How many times did Tony Dorsett rush for 100 yards or more in his rookie season?

38 Which two future Dallas Cowboys played in the 1966 College All-Star Game?

39 As a rookie for Minnesota he once returned a kickoff 101 yards.

40 In his best game as a rookie he scored three touchdowns against Cleveland in the Eastern Conference Championship. Who was he?

41 He was the second rookie to lead the Cowboys in rushing.

42 How many times did Duane Thomas run for 100 or more yards in his rookie year (during the regular season)?

43 This Cowboy was a member of the NFL All-Rookie team as a defensive end in 1961.

44 Why did Don Perkins have so much trouble with the Landry Mile when he came to training camp?

45 He was the highest NFL draft choice from Yale since 1969, when Calvin Hill was a first-round choice.

DALLAS COWBOYS TRIVIA **21** CHALLENGE CONTEST!

He played for the national collegiate champions in his senior year in college and for the Super Bowl champions his first year in the pros.

A. Larry Bethea. **B.** Tony Dorsett. **C.** Tody Smith. **D.** Bill Gregory.

---

rookie" in XIII?

46 What two quarterbacks were drafted by Dallas in 1965?

47 Who were the last two members of the Dirty Dozen to remain with the Cowboys?

48 The Cowboys have drafted only three interior offensive linemen in the first round. Name them.

49 Who was the first offensive lineman drafted No. 1 by the Cowboys and what year was he picked?

50 Which quarterback did the Cowboys draft as a future pick in 1962?

Rookie Everson Walls with his specialty — an interception.

51 His school dropped football his senior year, but he was drafted in the sixth round by the Cowboys in 1962.

52 What 6-7 quarterback did Dallas draft from TCU?

53 Who did the Cowboys pick in the draft with the choice they received from the New York Giants for Craig Morton?

drafted three Thomases. Name them.

62 Have the Cowboys ever drafted any brothers?

63 These three future Cowboys were teammates in 1964 at the North-South Shrine Game.

64 Who did Bob Lilly say he would have signed with if the Cowboys hadn't drafted him?

DALLAS COWBOYS TRIVIA **22** **CHALLENGE CONTEST!**

He skipped his senior year at Tulsa after being drafted as a future by the Cowboys.

A. Drew Pearson. **B.** Jerry Rhome. **C.** Willie Townes. **D.** Gary Porterfield.

---

54 Dallas drafted three quarterbacks in 1964. Who were they?

55 Which quarterback from Notre Dame did Dallas draft in 1969?

56 Who was the first quarterback from SMU drafted by Dallas?

57 A kidney injury in 1963 sidelined this rookie of the year candidate.

58 Who was the only rookie free agent to make the club in 1982?

65 What changed Roger Staubach's status five days before he reported to the Cowboys?

66 Later considered a washout, this No. 1 draft pick from Boston College was one of four running backs picked in the 1972 draft.

67 Who was the Cowboys' first No. 1 draft pick from Michigan?

68 This No. 2 pick from Virginia Tech had an outstanding senior year in col-

---

DALLAS COWBOYS TRIVIA **23** **CHALLENGE CONTEST!**

Dallas used the draft pick obtained for John Niland to draft this wide receiver.

A. Duke Fergerson. **B.** Tony Hill. **C.** Todd Christensen. **D.** Butch Johnson.

---

59 The Cowboys drafted these future Pro Bowl performers with the choices they received by trading Tody Smith and Billy Parks.

60 What happened to Dallas' first two draft picks in 1967?

61 In the early 1970s, the Cowboys

lege, with 65 tackles, five interceptions and two sacks.

69 He became the third rookie to lead the team in interceptions (in 1970).

70 This No. 1 draft pick started his college career in the Big Ten at 6-4 and 215 pounds, but was still growing at

6-7½ and 272 when Dallas picked him.

71 Who was the third Heisman trophy winner drafted by the Cowboys?

72 Which Dallas Heisman trophy-winning draft picks led their schools to national championships?

73 Before transferring to Florida, this Cowboy draft pick went to Western Arizona Junior College. He started 13 games at Florida and was a third-round draft pick.

74 In his rookie year, a 53-yard run against Houston helped him average better than six yards on 33 carries for the season.

75 This Cowboy draft pick finished his college career as Florida Tech's all-time leading scorer, runner, and pass receiver. He rushed for 4,066 yards, No. 17 on the NCAA's all-time list.

76 This draft pick held the Florida bench-press record with 515 pounds before being picked by the Cowboys.

Calvin Hill makes his patented escape.

DALLAS COWBOYS TRIVIA **24** CHALLENGE CONTEST!

Who was the punter from the Dirty Dozen?
A. Danny White. **B.** Mitch Hoopes. **C.** Jim Miller. **D.** Efren Herrera.

77 Who was the second Virginia Tech draft choice of 1985?

78 Who was Dallas' lone draft choice from the Southwest Conference in 1985?

79 Who was the Cowboys' draft choice from Maine in 1983?

80 Who were the Cowboys' "golden picks"?

81 Who were the consecutive draft choices from the same college in 1977?

82 He matched his Grambling school record for interceptions in his first year with the Cowboys.

83 Who was the Dirty Dozen defensive back from Boise State?

84 Which members of the Dirty Dozen were still with the Cowboys during the Silver Season?

85 Who was the only running back in the Dirty Dozen?

86 Name the other defensive back from the Dirty Dozen.

(THE ROOKIES — ANSWERS)

A **1** The Dirty Dozen.

2 He played on the special team in each game.

3 Ed (Too Tall) Jones.

4 Tony Dorsett and Los Angeles kicker Rafael Septien.

5 Yes. He was the punter in 1976.

6 Bob Hayes in 1965.

7 Burton Lawless was a starter as a rookie; Mitch Hoopes was the Cowboys' regular punter his first season.

8 Eleven (a 12th rookie, Percy Howard, was the other member of the Dirty Dozen . . . he was a free agent).

9 Preston Pearson, an NFL veteran free agent, and Warren Capone, a free agent from the World Football League.

10 Oklahoma (Randy Hughes and Kyle Davis) and Stanford (Scott Laidlaw and Pat Donovan).

11 Danny White.

12 Drew Pearson.

13 The 13th-round draft choice was only 20.

14 Billy Joe DuPree.

15 Harvey Martin.

16 No. In fact, he never carried the ball for Dallas. He returned two kickoffs in his only season with the Cowboys.

17 Doug Dennison (he carried 16 times and scored four times).

18 Ed (Too Tall) Jones.

19 Dennis Morgan — he returned the kick for a touchdown against St. Louis.

20 Randy White.

21 Butch Johnson in 1976 (he broke his own record each of the next two years).

22 Jay Saldi.

23 Danny White (with a 38.4 average — but he improved on it in each of the next three seasons).

24 Yes, Ricky Bell of Southern California was picked by the Tampa Bay Bucs.

25 Tony Dorsett.

26 In the 10th game of his rookie year.

27 Rookie Bruce Huther.

28 Rookie Bruce Thornton (with six).

29 Don Meredith in his rookie year, 1960.

30 Mel Renfro; seven of the returns were for 20 or more yards and two were good for more than 50.

31 Mel Renfro. He was No. 7 in the league with 40 returns for 1,017 yards and a 25.4-yard average.

32 Tony Dorsett. He scored on a 77-yard run against St. Louis and on an 84-yarder against Philadelphia.

33 Jackie Smith (he was making his first — and only — appearance in the game at age 38).

34 Mike Hagen. He got a tryout but didn't make the team.

35 Defensive back Woodley Lewis of Oregon. He played one year.

36 Don Talbert (an eighth-round future pick in 1961) from the University of Texas.

37 Twice, against St. Louis and Philadelphia.

38 John Niland and Walt Garrison.

39 Lance Rentzel, against Baltimore.

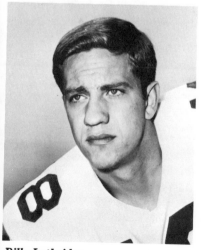

Billy Lothridge

40 Craig Baynham in 1967.

41 Calvin Hill, with 942 yards in 1969.

42 Five times (twice against Washington and once each against Houston, Detroit, and Kansas City).

43 Bob Lilly.

44 Perkins was 20 pounds over his college playing weight.

45 Jeff Rohrer. He was drafted in the second round of 1982.

46 Craig Morton and Ernie Kellerman.

47 Randy White and Mike Hegman.

48 John Niland, Robert Shaw, and Howard Richards.

49 John Niland in 1966.

50 Sonny Gibbs.

51 George Andrie from Marquette.

52 Guy (Sonny) Gibbs.

53 Randy White.

54 Billy Lothridge, Roger Staubach, and Jerry Rhome.

55 Bob Belden.

56 Keith Bobo.

57 Lee Roy Jordan.

58 Brian Baldinger.

59 Ed (Too Tall) Jones and Danny White.

60 They were sent to Houston as part of the settlement in the Ralph Neely affair.

61 Duane in 1970, Ike in 1971, and Bill in 1972.

62 Yes, Paul Brothers in 1967. Also, the Cowboys drafted Scott Pelluer in 1981 and his brother, Steve, in 1984; and Golden Richards in 1973 and his brother, Doug, in 1974.

63 Bob Hayes, Jerry Rhome, and Roger Staubach.

64 The Dallas Texans.

Gary Hogeboom cranks up his rifle arm.

Craig Baynham holds on for a few yards.

65 Don Meredith retired.

66 Bill Thomas.

67 Kevin Brooks in 1985.

68 Jesse Penn.

69 Charlie Waters.

70 Kevin Brooks.

71 Herschel Walker.

72 Herschel Walker and Tony Dorsett.

73 Crawford Ker.

74 Charles Young.

75 Robert Lavette.

76 Crawford Ker.

77 Joe Jones.

78 Matt Darwin from A&M.

79 Running back Lorenzo Bouier.

80 Dennis Golden in 1963 and Golden Richards in 1973.

81 Guy Brown and Val Belcher from Houston.

82 Everson Walls. He intercepted 11 passes.

83 Rolly Woolsey.

84 Herb Scott, Bob Breunig, Randy White, and Mike Hegman.

85 Scott Laidlaw.

86 Randy Hughes.

BOWLING FOR DOLLARS

Several members of the Dallas Cowboys distinguished themselves in college bowl games before joining the pro ranks. Others have made names for themselves as All-Pro performers and by participating in the Pro Bowl. None have made second careers on the professional bowlers tour, however.

Q

1 He scored a 39-yard touchdown on an end-around in the 1964 North-South Shrine Bowl game.

2 This former Cowboy was named the Most Valuable Player in the 1964 North-South Shrine Bowl.

3 He was a four-year starter at Florida State — and played in four bowl games.

4 This player began his college career as a freshman against Georgia — and ended it in a bowl game against the same team.

5 This future Cowboy played on the winning team in the 1961 Orange Blossom Classic Bowl game.

6 When was Buck Buchanan first named National Football Conference equipment manager for the Pro Bowl?

7 Who was the Cowboys' only offensive player in the 1966 Pro Bowl?

8 In the same game, Dallas had five players on the defensive unit for the East. Who were they?

9 Which two Cowboys made their first Pro Bowl appearances in the 1967 game?

10 As a member of the Pittsburgh Steelers, he once participated in eight straight Pro Bowl games.

Chuck Howley was a repeat selection on the All-Pro list in the '60s.

DALLAS COWBOYS TRIVIA **25** CHALLENGE CONTEST!

Who threw the first touchdown pass for the Cowboys in the "Ice Bowl"?

A. Roger Staubach. **B.** Dan Reeves. **C.** Calvin Hill. **D.** Don Perkins.

11 How many passes did Everson Walls intercept in his first Pro Bowl game?

12 He was with the Cleveland Browns for two years and the Los Angeles Rams for a year before coming to Dallas. In college, he played on the University of Texas' 1958 Sugar Bowl team and 1960 Cotton Bowl club. Who was he?

13 Which three Cowboys played in the Pro Bowl for the first time in 1979?

14 These two future Cowboys were dismissed from the Oklahoma team before the 1965 Gator Bowl for signing pro contracts.

15 He made 21 tackles against Oklahoma in the 1963 Orange Bowl.

16 This Cowboy had 81- and 54-yard touchdown interception returns in the 1971 Pro Bowl.

17 Who was the first kicker to play in the Pro Bowl representing the Dallas Cowboys?

18 Who was the first Cowboy to score a touchdown in the Pro Bowl?

19 What two bowls did Tom Landry help his team, the University of Texas, win his last two years of college?

20 What was called the Neely Bowl?

21 He was All-Southwest Conference his junior year and helped his team beat Alabama in the Sugar Bowl.

22 In which stadium did Roger Staubach fail to win a game during his Heisman trophy season at Navy?

DALLAS COWBOYS TRIVIA **26** **CHALLENGE CONTEST!**

Who played in the Pro Bowl his rookie year and ran back an interception for a touchdown?

A. Cliff Harris.   **B.** Mel Renfro.   **C.** Charlie Waters.   **D.** Everson Walls.

Mel Renfro seems to be enjoying this tug of war between assistant coaches Ermal Allen (left) and Dick Nolan.

(BOWLING FOR DOLLARS — ANSWERS)

 1 Bob Hayes.

2 Bob Hayes, of course.

3 Larry Brinson.

4 Tony Dorsett.

5 Bob Hayes.

6 In 1973.

7 Bob Hayes.

8 George Andrie, Bob Lilly, Mel Renfro, Cornell Green, and Chuck Howley were named to the 1969 defensive unit of the East squad for the Pro Bowl.

9 Dave Manders and Don Meredith.

10 Assistant coach Ernie Stautner.

11 Two.

12 Larry Stephens.

13 Thomas Henderson, Tony Hill, and Tony Dorsett.

14 Ralph Neely and Lance Rentzel.

15 Lee Roy Jordan.

16 Mel Renfro.

17 Sam Baker.

18 Dick Bielski.

19 The Sugar Bowl in 1948 and the Cotton Bowl in 1949.

20 The annual pre-season game between Dallas and Houston.

21 Tom Landry.

22 The Cotton Bowl. Staubach was the quarterback at Navy, where the Midshipmen lost to SMU in the Cotton Bowl in the regular season and to Texas in the Cotton Bowl game.

Bob Hayes takes a tumble for a good cause — another catch.

WHAT'S IN A NAME?

The Cowboys are known as "America's Team," Bob Hayes was known as the "Bullet" . . . nicknames are a part of all sports. But what about "Rocky," "Joe Palooka," and "The Hammer"? They were also key players for the Dallas Cowboys.

Q

1 What was the name of the Clemson backfield when Chuck McSwain played for the Tigers?

2 What is Monty Hunter's first name?

3 Which Dallas defensive back was nicknamed "Bird"?

4 Who was the famous freeloader-gate-crasher who spent the entire summer with the Cowboys at their first training camp?

5 Who is the rookies' "godfather"?

6 What is Dextor Clinkscale's first name?

7 What is Rafael Septien's first name?

8 Who celebrated touchdowns with the "California quake"?

9 Who was "Pooch"?

10 His home town of Williamsburg, Va., named a street after him.

11 This 1984 draft pick was nicknamed "Sweetback."

12 What was the nickname given to the Cowboys' defense in the mid-1960s

— and what was the revised name in the late '70s?

13 His home town is known as "home of the grapefruit."

H.R. Bright

57

14 Who were the last two members of the "Beau Geste" squad?

15 Who was nicknamed "Pop" his last few years at training camp?

16 Who gave himself the nickname "Still Bill"?

17 Who was nicknamed "Long Gone"?

18 What was Babe Dimancheff's first name?

34 Who was nicknamed "Todzilla"?

35 What was "Wings of Victory"?

36 Who was "Buzz"?

37 What was "Buzz" short for?

38 Who was nicknamed "Bullwinkle"?

39 This offensive lineman was nicknamed "Dog."

40 Who gave himself the nickname "Baby Cakes"?

DALLAS COWBOYS TRIVIA **28** **CHALLENGE CONTEST!**

What was the name of the Tyler Junior College group that performed at Cowboy halftimes?

A. The Roses. **B.** The Troubadeers. **C.** The Apache Belles. **D.** The Tyler Troopers.

---

19 What is Butch Johnson's full name?

20 Who was nicknamed "Utility Man"?

21 What was Cliff Harris' nickname?

22 Who was nicknamed "Strip"?

23 What was "ProMotion"?

24 What is Charlie Waters' middle name?

25 Who were "Charlie's Angels"?

26 Who was the first Cornhusker to play for Dallas?

27 Who was nicknamed "Speed-O"?

28 What was the name of the highlight film of the Cowboys' 1977 Super Bowl championship season?

29 Who was nicknamed "Spur"?

30 What is Tex Schramm's real first name?

31 How did Tex Schramm get his name?

32 Who was known in school as "the Crow"?

33 How did Bob Hayes get the nickname "World's Fastest Human"?

41 What was Roger Staubach's 50-yard desperation pass to Drew Pearson in the 1975 playoffs against Minnesota known as?

BOB HAYES • WR

No. 22 on the program and No. 1 in your hearts.

42 What is H.R. Bright's nickname?

43 What did the Cowboys use as the theme to the 25th anniversary season?

44 How many Cowboys earned the right to the nickname "World's Fastest Human"?

45 What name did Tom Landry give Larry Cole after his last touchdown return against the Washington Redskins?

46 Which Cowboy played on the same East Texas State team as "Mad Dog"?

47 This offensive guard was nicknamed "Jiggs."

48 He was nicknamed "Moose."

49 This Cowboys player from the early years was nicknamed "Forward."

It's a dirty job, but Jethro Pugh did it from 1965-78.

Amos Marsh

50 What was the name of the Cowboy figure on the horse used on Dallas Cowboys material in the early 1960s?

51 Who nicknamed Danny White "America's Punter"?

52 Who was known as "Rocky"?

53 He answered to the nickname "Joe Palooka."

54 Who was known as "Bubba" for the Cowboys?

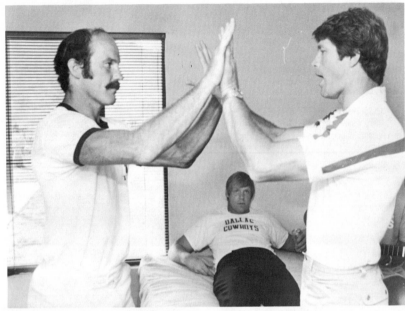

Patty-cake, patty-cake for Cliff Harris (left) and Charlie Waters. A bored Larry Cole looks on.

DALLAS COWBOYS TRIVIA **29** CHALLENGE CONTEST!

This longtime Cowboy tight end was known by his initials.

A. Mike Ditka (MD). **B.** Jim Jensen (JJ). **C.** Billy Joe DuPree (BJ). **D.** Pettis Norman (PN).

---

55 Who was known as "The Hammer" on the Cowboys' squad?

56 What did the term "swing team" mean to the Cowboys in 1960?

57 What was the name of the game in which the Cowboys made their home debut in 1960?

58 What was "A Champion in Waiting"?

59 Who were "the Hoopsters"?

60 Who was known as "the Bullet"?

61 How did the Cowboys come by their "America's Team" tag in 1978?

62 What was the nickname originally chosen for the Cowboys?

63 Why did Dallas change its nickname to Cowboys in 1960?

64 Who was referred to as "Fair and Square"?

65 Who was "Hollywood"?

66 Who was called "the Dodger"?

67 Who played on the line of the original "Doomsday Defense"?

68 Who was "Dandy?"

69 Who was "Bubba's" little brother?

70 Who was the "Mad Bomber"?

71 Who was "Bambi"?

72 Who were the original members of the "Zero Club"?

73 What was the nickname for Cleveland Jones?

74 Who was "J.R."?

75 Who was "Little O"?

someone in the Cowboys' front office.

86 What was the name of the Oklahoma team that Cowboy taxi squad members played for in the 1970s?

87 Who was nicknamed "Suitcase"?

88 Who nicknamed Craig Morton "Curley"?

89 Who is "Cubby"?

90 What is the name of the development that is home for the Cowboys' new headquarters?

DALLAS COWBOYS TRIVIA **30** **CHALLENGE CONTEST!**

Who was the "Purple Cloud"?

A. Tony Dorsett.　　**B.** Bob Hayes.　　**C.** Bob Lilly.　　**D.** Rayfield Wright.

---

76 Who was "Big Tom"?

77 Who was "Too Mean"?

78 What Cowboy was nicknamed "Thrill"?

79 What is Tom Landry's middle name?

80 Who is nicknamed the "Manster"?

81 Who was called "Captain America"?

82 Who was nicknamed "Abner"?

83 This "Zero Club" member was a former high school quarterback.

84 What broadcaster nicknamed L. G. Dupre "Long Gone"?

85 This early-day kick return specialist shared the same last name as

91 Who was "Onside"?

92 Who was called "Puddin"?

93 Who is the "Hawk"?

94 What is Harvey Martin's middle name?

95 Who was nicknamed "A.M.-P.M."?

96 Who is called "Mr. Cowboy"?

97 What was "Back in the Saddle Again"?

98 What were the first Cowboys cheerleaders called?

99 What did the Cowboys call their 25th Anniversary celebration at the Registry Hotel?

DALLAS COWBOYS TRIVIA **31** **CHALLENGE CONTEST!**

Who gave the "Manster" his nickname?

A. Charlie Waters.　**B.** Cliff Harris.　**C.** Harvey Martin.　**D.** Randy White.

DALLAS COWBOYS TRIVIA **32** **CHALLENGE CONTEST!**

This kickoff return specialist, nicknamed "Strawberry," had more than 1,100 yards in his only year with the Cowboys.

A. Gary Allen. **B.** Ike Thomas. **C.** Dennis Morgan. **D.** Louie Walker.

---

100 What was the name given the dessert at the 25th Anniversary celebration dinner?

101 Who was "the House"?

102 Who was called "White Lightning"?

103 What do the initials in D.D. Lewis stand for?

104 Who coined the name "Doomsday Defense"?

105 This Dallas player was the first Cowboy to be known as "The Boomer."

106 Who was "the Sphinx"?

(WHAT'S IN A NAME — ANSWERS)

1 The "McBackfield" (Jeff McCall was the fullback).

2 Orie.

3 Ron Fellows.

4 "Jungle Jamey."

5 Gil Brandt.

6 Frederick.

7 Jose.

8 Butch Johnson.

9 Herb Scott.

10 Ron Springs (Ron Springs Drive).

11 Mike Revell.

12 The "Doomsday Defense" led the Cowboys in the '60s — and in the '70s it became "Doomsday II" or "Doomsday Jr."

13 Tom Landry — his home town is Mission, Texas.

14 Don Meredith and Mike Connelly.

15 Roger Staubach.

16 Bill Gregory.

17 L.G. Dupre.

18 Boris.

19 Michael McColly Johnson.

20 Jim Cooper.

21 "Captain Crash."

22 Mark Washington.

23 Charlie Waters' talent agency.

24 Tutan.

25 Members of the defensive secondary during the early 1980s — headed by Charlie Waters.

26 Ed Hussman of Nebraska (in 1970).

27 Bob Hayes.

28 "The Year the Clock Struck XII."

29 Danny Spradlin.

30 Texas.

31 His father didn't want him to forget his Texas roots.

32 Bob Hayes — because he could fly in track or on the football field.

33 By winning the Olympic 100 meters.

34 Todd Christensen.

35 The name Tony Hill gave to his touchdown celebration.

36 Jethro Pugh.

37 "Buzzard."

38 George Andrie.

39 Dave Manders.

40 Willie Townes.

41 The "Hail Mary TD."

42 "Bum."

43 They called it the "Silver Season."

44 Just one — Bob Hayes. Dallas drafted 1984 Olympic sprint champ Carl Lewis, but Lewis chose not to sign with Dallas.

Thomas Henderson

45 "The Galloping Ghost."

46 Harvey Martin ("Mad Dog" was Pittsburgh's Dwight White).

47 Andy Cvercko.

48 Amos Marsh.

49 Amos Marsh.

50 Cowboy Joe.

51 Roger Staubach.

52 Jim Colvin.

53 Larry Cole.

54 Again — Larry Cole.

55 Mike Ditka (he got the nickname for basketball play in college).

56 It meant Dallas would be listed in the Western Conference in its first year — but would play every other team in each conference once, instead of playing most of its games within the conference.

57 The Salesmanship Club game.

58 The name of the Cowboys' 1974 highlight film.

59 The Cowboys' winter basketball team.

60 Bob Hayes.

61 NFL Films chose it as the title for a motion picture of the team's highlights.

62 The Rangers.

63 There was already a minor-league baseball team named Rangers in the Dallas-Fort Worth area.

64 Roger Staubach.

65 Thomas Henderson.

66 Roger Staubach.

67 Willie Townes, Bob Lilly, Jethro Pugh, and George Andrie.

68 Don Meredith.

69 Tody, who was with the Cowboys two years. He was the brother of Bubba Smith.

70 Clint Longley.

71 Lance Alworth.

72 Larry Cole, Blaine Nye, and Pat Toomay.

73 "Pussyfoot."

74 Rafael Septien's parrot, named after "Jose Rafael" Septien.

75 Obert Logan.

76 Rayfield Wright.

77 That was the nickname given Harvey Martin when he was a defensive linemate of Ed "Too Tall" Jones. However, Martin did not care for the name.

78 Tony "The Thrill" Hill.

79 Wade.

80 The half-man, half-monster — Randy White.

81 Roger Staubach.

82 Bob Lilly.

83 Pat Toomay.

84 Kern Tips.

85 Ola Lee Murchison.

86 Oklahoma City Plainsmen.

87 Paul Dickson (because of his large hands).

88 Don Meredith.

89 Everson Walls.

90 Valley Ranch.

91 Kicker Mike Clark.

92 Walt Garrison.

93 Tony Dorsett.

94 Banks.

95 Aaron Mitchell.

96 Bob Lilly.

97 The name of the record put out by Firestone highlighting the 1977 season.

98 Belles and Beaux.

99 The Silver Soiree.

100 Baked Doomsday.

101 Robert Newhouse.

102 Doug Donley.

103 Dwight Douglas.

104 Former Dallas Morning News sportswriter Gary Cartwright.

105 Colin Ridgway.

106 Duane Thomas.

Bob Lilly's friends and admirers called him "Mister."

Colin Ridgway gets a 40-yard checkup from kicking coach Ben Agajanian.

THE NUMBERS GAME

Numbers play a big part in pro football, on the scoreboard, on the field — and lately in salary negotiations. You already know, of course, that the Cowboys have had only "one" head coach in 26 years, have won "two" Super Bowls and have had "three" players named Hill play for them. There are plenty of other numbers in the Cowboys' past, present, and future.

Don Meredith gets the play from Tom Landry as John Roach (right) listens to the strategy.

1 Beginning in 1961, how many consecutive years did Green Bay play Dallas in the Salesmanship Club game?

2 How many times have the Cowboys been shut out in regular-season and playoff games?

3 What is the significance of the numbers 12-8-64?

4 He became the Cowboys' No. 2 quarterback when Craig Morton was traded.

5 What was the score in the last meeting between the Dallas Cowboys and a George Allen-coached Washington Redskins team?

6 How many total points did the Cowboys allow in the two playoff games prior to Super Bowl XII?

7 How many other teams were in the National Football League when the Cowboys began play in 1960?

8 Tom Landry is credited with being one of the architects of the 4-3. What is the 4-3?

9 This former 1,000-yard rusher for the New York Giants failed to make it with the Cowboys in 1976.

10 His 542 rushing yards in 1976 was the lowest club-leading total since 1960.

11 How many players picked in the first four rounds of the 1975 draft made the team?

12 What year did Roger Staubach pass Craig Morton for second place on the Cowboys' all-time passing yards list?

13 During their 10 straight victories in 1971 (including three playoff games), the Cowboys were plus 22 in turnovers. How many takeaways did they have over that span?

14 Which three players were holders for Rafael Septien in 1979?

15 Who was the ninth player to rush for 100 or more yards in a single game?

16 How many times did Mel Renfro score on plays of 50 yards or more?

17 Only four Cowboys played 14 seasons for Dallas. Name them.

18 He was second in consecutive games played to Bob Lilly.

19 How many touchdown passes were thrown in the Cowboys' first regular-season game?

20 He averaged 6.8 yards rushing on 26 end arounds over his career.

D.D. Lewis

DALLAS COWBOYS TRIVIA 33 CHALLENGE CONTEST!

He was No. 2 on the team in rushing, scoring, and receiving in 1972.
A. Calvin Hill. **B.** Walt Garrison. **C.** Billy Parks. **D.** Mike Montgomery.

21 How many first downs did the Cowboys have in their first game?

22 In 1960, three of his nine pass receptions went for touchdowns — two for more than 70 yards. Who was he?

23 How many interceptions did Eddie LeBaron throw in the first regular-season Cowboys game?

24 Jim Brown gained 942 yards in his first pro season. Did Calvin Hill gain more or less in his rookie year?

25 He led the team in kickoff and punt returns in 1976 and combined for 1,182 yards in the two categories.

26 He tied for eighth in the NFC in kickoff returns in 1977 with 17 (for a 24.1-yard average).

27 Tampa Bay was the victim of his 79-yard interception return for a touchdown in 1977.

28 In 17 games (including the playoffs) in 1977, how many times did Roger Staubach fail to throw a touchdown pass?

29 What is the Cowboys' record for consecutive victories at Texas Stadium (regular season and playoffs combined)?

30 Larry Cole intercepted passes during each of his first two seasons. How many years went by before he added another steal?

31 He went from 21 receiving yards in his first year — to 823 in his second.

32 They shared the club lead in quarterback traps in 1978 (with 16 each).

33 How many games did Robert Newhouse miss in 1978 after he suffered a broken bone in his leg?

34 He broke his own record for receptions by a running back with 47 in 1978.

35 What year did Danny White finally lift his punting average over 40 yards per kick?

36 How many years did it take Tony Dorsett to move into the No. 5 spot on the Dallas Cowboys' all-time career rushing list?

37 In his fifth year, he finally led the team in interceptions with five in 1978. Who was he?

38 Preston Pearson led Dallas in receiving in 1978. How many touchdowns did he score?

39 How many seasons did it take Rafael Septien to pass Bob Hayes in career scoring?

A touchdown reception by Butch Johnson.

DALLAS COWBOYS TRIVIA **34** **CHALLENGE CONTEST!**

He was the first player to lead the team in passing for eight seasons.

A. Eddie LeBaron. **B.** Craig Morton. **C.** Roger Staubach. **D.** Danny White.

Quarterback Eddie LeBaron teams up with kicker Sam Baker.

40 How long did it take Everson Walls to move into the top 10 on Dallas' all-time career interception list?

41 Name the four Cowboys who carried the ball more than 1,000 times in their careers.

42 Which AFL team made Craig Morton its No. 1 draft pick?

43 How many different teams has Tony Dorsett gained 100 yards against in a single game?

44 How many times did Tony Dorsett rush for 100 or more yards in a single game against St. Louis in his first five years?

45 In his first six years, Tony Dorsett gained 1,000 yards against this team.

46 When was Tony Hill's first 1,000-yard season?

47 When was Ron Springs' first 1,000-yard season?

48 Which three backs drafted by the Cowboys in 1980 made the team?

49 Dallas had 24 first downs — the most against an opponent in the first year — against which team?

50 In what position did the Cowboys finish the first year they played in the Eastern Conference?

51 This Cowboy QB threw five interceptions in a single game in both 1960 and '61.

52 This one-time Cowboy once attempted seven field goals in a single game against Dallas (in 1960) and made six PATs in a single game for Dallas (in 1962). Name him.

53 He completed 10 straight pass attempts in 1963.

54 He caught passes in 34 straight games from 1960 through '63.

55 These two Dallas running backs combined for 1,747 rushing yards in '62.

56 In his record-setting 1981 season, how many times did Tony Dorsett run for more than 100 yards in a single game?

57 How many passes did Benny Barnes catch in his Cowboy career?

58 Tony Hill equaled his 1979 reception total in 1980. How many passes did he catch each season?

DALLAS COWBOYS TRIVIA **35** CHALLENGE CONTEST!

His career interception total is second only to Mel Renfro — and is the same as his jersey number.

A. Charlie Waters. **B.** Lee Roy Jordan. **C.** Chuck Howley. **D.** Cliff Harris.

59 How many 200-yard games did Danny White have in his first year as the Cowboys' starting quarterback?

60 How many games did Tom Landry win during the 10-year period from 1970 through 1979, compared to Don Shula?

61 How long did it take the Cowboys to win a game in their rivalry with the Washington Redskins?

62 How many consecutive starts did Billy Joe DuPree make between 1976 and '81 before Doug Cosbie won the starting tight end job?

63 In Tony Dorsett's first 44 games in which he ran for 100 yards or more, how many times did the Cowboys win?

64 What is Randy White's record bench press?

65 Who threw more interceptions, Roger Staubach or Don Meredith?

66 He ran for 101 yards in his first college varsity game, against the University of Georgia.

67 What was the score in the first game that Tony Dorsett started as a pro?

68 How many touchdowns did Tony Dorsett score in the regular season in his first year as a pro?

69 What is the significance of April 7, 1954?

70 How many times did Bob Lilly make All-Pro?

71 He was rated the No. 12 offensive tackle in the nation by the "Winline Sports Service 1982 Draft Report."

72 What was the Cowboys' record in 1971 when Tom Landry finally named Roger Staubach to start over Craig Morton?

73 Before the famous Hail Mary touchdown pass by Roger Staubach, where did Dallas start the drive in that game against Minnesota?

74 What rookie quarterback was listed at 6-6 (two inches more than his actual height) in the Cowboy media guide?

75 How many regular-season games did Bob Lilly miss in his Dallas career?

76 In 1979, he caught 17 third-down passes and converted 16 of them into first downs. Name him.

77 He was a three-time Little All-American quarterback.

78 He was featured on the first four Cowboys media guides.

DALLAS COWBOYS TRIVIA **36** CHALLENGE CONTEST!

He was the Cowboys' defensive leader in 1960 with 47 tackles and 101 assists.

A. Bob Lilly. **B.** Jerry Tubbs. **C.** Jack Patera. **D.** Jack Sherer.

DALLAS COWBOYS TRIVIA **37** **CHALLENGE CONTEST!**

The Cowboys had two players in the NFL's top 10 in scoring in 1962. Who were they?

A. Don Perkins and Don Meredith.   **B.** Don Perkins and Bob Hayes.
C. Sam Baker and Bob Hayes.   **D.** Frank Clarke and Sam Baker.

Danny Reeves conveys a message.

79 He was the Cowboys' No. 4 rusher in 1961 and had an eight-yard per-carry average.

80 He gained exactly one mile rushing his first two seasons.

81 The Cowboys had two rushers in the NFL's top 10 in 1962. Who were they?

82 How many snaps did Sonny Gibbs take in 1963?

83 This cornerback was rated No. 9 at his position by "Winline Sports Service 1982 Draft Report."

84 He was only seventh in the league in average, but led the NFL in number and yards in kickoff return statistics in 1964.

85 Name the five future Cowboys who played in the 1965 College All-Star game against the NFL champions.

86 What year did Billy Howton catch his 500th career pass?

87 How did Don Meredith and Bob Hayes rank among league passing and receiving leaders in 1966?

88 Dan Reeves was listed in six statistical categories for the Cowboys in 1966. What were they?

89 In 1966, how many times did Don Meredith pass for four or more touchdowns in a single game?

90 The Cowboys almost had two 1,000-yard receivers as early as 1967. Who were the near-miss receivers?

91 He was only the third linebacker picked by the Cowboys in the 1968 draft — but he made the team.

92 He was the third Cowboy to rush for more than 100 yards in a single game. Name him.

93 How many passes did Calvin Hill complete in his rookie year?

94 How long after Don Meredith retired did Don Perkins announce he was quitting football?

95 How many 1,000-yard seasons did Lance Alworth have at San Diego before he came to the Cowboys?

96 In 1970, Dallas scored six points or less three times. Did the Cowboys win any of those games?

DALLAS COWBOYS TRIVIA **38** CHALLENGE CONTEST!

How many times did Dallas win the Capitol Division?

A. None.   **B.** Once in three years.   **C.** Twice in three years.
D. All three years.

---

97 Roger Staubach started 17 games in his first three years with the Cowboys. How many did Dallas win?

98 What was the first season the Cowboys didn't have a passer ranked in the NFL's top 10?

99 This Cowboy's number wasn't retired, but hasn't been used since '74.

100 Benny Barnes scored the first touchdown of his Cowboy career on a 33-yard fumble return. How did he score his only other TD?

101 He caught 106 passes and led Ohio State in receiving for four years.

102 They shared the team lead in interceptions in 1980.

103 Which Cowboys game was named one of the top 10 "greatest days in Texas sports history" in a Texas Sports Hall of Fame writers poll?

104 Who scored more points in 1984, the Cowboys or their opponents?

105 Three players threw touchdown passes for Dallas in 1984. Danny White and Gary Hogeboom were the first two. Who was the third?

106 How many individual 100-yard rushing games did Dallas backs produce in 1984?

107 What happened to Sam Baker in his first year in Dallas when he missed the team plane after an exhibition game?

108 Who was the Cowboys' leading touchdown scorer in 1960?

109 These two 1984 starters have the same birthday as President Reagan.

110 The Cowboys set a club scoring record in 1983 with 479 points. Did they lead the league?

111 He played in only four games — and touched the ball only four times — in 1978, but scored two touchdowns.

112 What two Cowboys won Super Bowl MVP awards and wore the same jersey number?

113 Who was the first Cowboy to wear No. 13?

114 Which two quarterbacks wore No. 14 before Gary Hogeboom?

115 Two wide receivers and a quarterback wore No. 19. Name them.

116 His uniform number (43) was retired at New Mexico.

117 Tony Dorsett matched his college jersey number with the number of career collegiate 100-yard rushing games. What was the number?

118 This kicker was the only Cowboy to wear the number 38.

119 Both Chuck Howley and Randy White made jersey No. 54 famous. Who was the first Cowboy to wear that number?

120 How many times did Roger Staubach pass for more than 400 yards in a single game?

121 What Cowboy tight end wore No. 89 before Billy Joe DuPree?

122 Beginning in 1982, Jeff Rohrer wore No. 50. What two linebackers wore the number before Rohrer?

123 He was the first Cowboy to wear No. 26 who didn't come from another NFL team.

124 Roger Staubach made it famous, but who was the first to wear No. 12 for Dallas?

125 Who was the first Cowboy to wear No. 3?

126 The first two Cowboys to wear No. 10 were punters. Who were they?

127 A placekicker and a quarterback wore No. 15. Name them.

128 What two Cowboy backs made All-Pro and wore jersey No. 43?

(THE NUMBERS GAME — ANSWERS)

A

1 Ten — before New Orleans was the opponent in 1971.

2 Four times: by St. Louis in regular-season play in 1970, by Los Angeles in the 1969 Playoff Bowl, by Chicago in the 1985 regular season, and by the Rams in the 1985 playoffs.

3 December 8, 1964, is the day Bob Hayes signed with Dallas.

4 Clint Longley.

5 Dallas won, 14-7.

6 Thirteen; they beat Chicago, 33-7, and Minnesota, 23-6.

7 Twelve; the Cowboys played each team once their first year.

8 The defensive alignment with four down linemen and three linebackers.

9 Ron Johnson.

10 Doug Dennison.

11 Six (Dallas had two picks in both the first and fourth rounds).

12 In 1975, his seventh.

13 An amazing 34.

14 Glenn Carano, Danny White, and Charlie Waters.

15 Scott Laidlaw (vs. Philadelphia in 1976).

16 Four (two on kickoff returns, one on a punt return, and one on an interception).

17 D.D. Lewis, Jethro Pugh, Lee Roy Jordan, and Bob Lilly.

18 Cornell Green (with 168 games).

19 Eight (five by the opponent and three by Dallas).

20 Billy Joe DuPree.

21 Seventeen.

22 Frank Clarke.

23 Three.

24 He gained the same number as Brown.

25 Butch Johnson (489 on punt returns and 693 on kickoff runbacks).

26 Larry Brinson.

27 Thomas (Hollywood) Henderson.

28 Only twice.

29 Eighteen games (all games played there in 1980 and '81; Dallas lost the last game of '79 and the first in '82).

30 Nine.

31 Tony Hill.

32 Harvey Martin and Randy White.

33 Only three.

34 Preston Pearson.

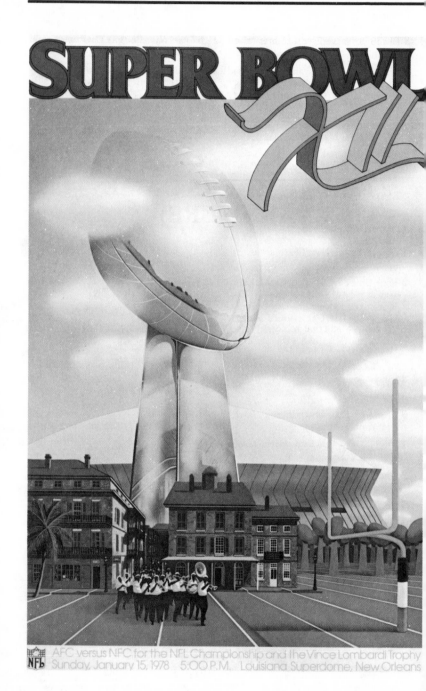

35 In 1978; he averaged 40.5 in his third year.

36 Less than two (27 games); he passed Amos Marsh for fifth.

37 Benny Barnes.

38 None, even though he caught 47 passes.

39 Septien passed Hayes in five years and has been adding to his career record ever since.

40 Two seasons (it took everyone else on the list at least six).

41 Tony Dorsett, Don Perkins, Calvin Hill, and Robert Newhouse.

42 The Oakland Raiders.

43 Twenty-one.

44 Five.

45 St. Louis. He had 1,006 yards in 11 games. In addition to the five 100-yard games, he had a 99-yard effort and another for 98 yards.

46 In 1979 (he caught 60 passes for 1,062 yards).

47 In 1979. He rushed for 248, caught passes for 251 and returned kickoffs for 780 — a total of 1,279.

48 Gary Hogeboom, James Jones, and Timmy Newsome.

49 Detroit.

50 Sixth (in a seven-team conference).

51 Eddie LeBaron. His negative record has been tied only once.

52 Sam Baker. He still holds several records, both for and against Dallas.

53 Don Meredith.

54 Billy Howton.

55 Don Perkins (945 yards) and Amos Marsh (802).

56 Nine times (twice against Washington and once against Miami, Philadelphia, New England, St. Louis, Los Angeles, Baltimore, and Buffalo).

57 He caught two for a total of 80 yards.

58 Sixty.

59 Ten (including eight in a row from the second through ninth games).

60 He won 105; Shula won 104.

61 Five games (the Redskins won two of the first four and two others were ties).

62 He had 93.

63 Dallas won 41.

64 He's gone over the 500-pound mark (501).

65 Meredith threw 111; Staubach had 109.

66 Tony Dorsett.

67 Pittsburgh 28, Dallas 13. It was the 10th game of 1977. Dorsett had 73 yards rushing.

68 He scored 12 in the regular season and four in three playoff games.

69 That's Tony Dorsett's birthday.

70 Seven.

71 Phil Pozderac.

72 Dallas was 4-3 at the time.

73 At its own 15-yard line.

74 Craig Morton.

75 None.

76 Preston Pearson.

77 Eddie LeBaron.

78 Cowboy Joe.

79 Don Meredith.

80 Don Perkins (815 yards his first year and 945 his second for a total of 1,760).

81 Don Perkins (fifth) and Amos Marsh (seventh).

82 One, during the pre-season.

83 Rod Hill.

84 Mel Renfro with 40 returns for 1,017 yards.

85 Russell Wayt, Malcolm Walker, Bob Hayes, Ralph Neely, and Craig Morton.

86 In 1963, his last with the Cowboys.

87 Each ranked fourth.

88 Rushing, receiving, passing, scoring, punt returns, and kickoff returns.

89 Three.

90 Bob Hayes had 998 yards and Lance Rentzel 996.

91 D.D. Lewis — Ed Harmon and John Douglas, the first two picks, failed to make the team.

92 Dan Reeves (vs. Cleveland in 1967). He had 114 on 18 carries.

93 Three (and two went for touchdowns).

94 Just 13 days.

95 Seven (from 1963 through '69).

96 Yes, two (6-2 over Cleveland in the regular season and 5-0 over Detroit in the playoffs).

97 Sixteen. The only loss was to St. Louis in 1970.

98 In 1964 (Don Meredith only had a 67.3 rating).

99 Bob Lilly; his number was 74.

100 On a 72-yard fumble return in 1980.

101 Doug Donley.

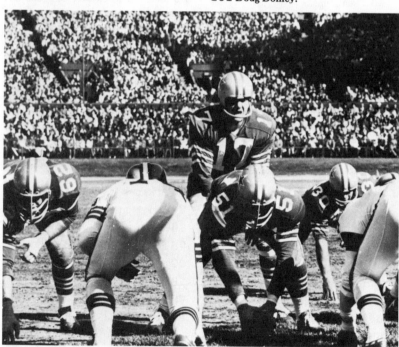

Don Meredith barks the signals in a 1969 contest against the Cleveland Browns.

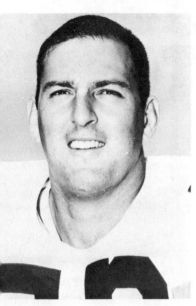

Mike Connelly

Jerry Tubbs

102 Dennis Thurman and Charlie Waters with five each.

103 Dallas' 24-3 Super Bowl victory over Miami in 1971.

104 Dallas scored 309 and allowed the same number.

105 Mike Renfro.

106 Only one, Tony Dorsett against Indianapolis (104 yards).

107 He caught a later plane, but still was fined $1,000.

108 L.G. Dupre with five.

109 John Dutton and Doug Donley.

110 No, Washington scored 541.

111 Jay Saldi (two of his three receptions were for scores).

112 Chuck Howley and Randy White both wore No. 54.

113 Jerry Rhome.

114 Eddie LeBaron and Craig Morton.

115 Lance Rentzel and Lance Alworth were the receivers; Clint Longley was the quarterback.

116 Don Perkins.

117 33.

118 Sam Baker.

119 Mike Connelly.

120 None.

121 Mike Ditka.

122 Jerry Tubbs and D.D. Lewis.

123 Michael Downs.

124 John Roach.

125 Jim Miller.

126 Ron Widby and Duane Carrell.

127 Tony Fritsch and Brad Wright.

128 Don Perkins and Cliff Harris.

I'D RATHER SWITCH

The Dallas Cowboys have a long history of drafting athletes who played little or no football ... then converting them into top-ranked professionals. Other teams marvel at the Cowboys' fortunes in turning college basketball players into top receivers or defensive backs. Dallas also has had success turning offensive linemen into defensive players ... and making numerous other switches.

Q

1 Former Oregon running back Mel Renfro was given a chance at a new position in 1966. What was it?

2 Which non-NFL city has hosted the most Cowboy pre-season games?

3 He came to the Cowboys as a free-agent basketball player from Michigan State in 1964.

4 Before distinguishing himself as a Cowboys receiver, he was a sprinter at Oregon. He signed as a free agent in 1962.

5 What was Randy White's first position with the Cowboys?

6 Before he became All-Pro as a defensive tackle, Randy White tried still another position. What was it?

7 Who was Don Meredith's successor at quarterback after Meredith's unexpected announcement that he was retiring?

8 This former super scout worked for Dallas from 1966 to 1970 before joining the New England Patriots.

9 Which team replaced New York in the Capitol Division in 1969 to become a division opponent of the Cowboys?

10 What makes Calvin Hill's 1972 Topps football card unusual?

11 A former quarterback in college, he spent a year as the No. 3 signal-caller for Dallas, even though he was one of the team's top running backs of all time.

12 Who alternated with Pettis Norman as a messenger in 1970?

13 This receiver's career was sandwiched between stops in the Canadian Football League and the World Football League.

14 He replaced Cliff Harris when Harris was called to military duty.

DALLAS COWBOYS TRIVIA **39** **CHALLENGE CONTEST!**

This offensive lineman was once a bodyguard for entertainer Ricky Nelson.

A. John Niland.   **B.** Blaine Nye.   **C.** Jim Boecke.   **D.** Rocky Colvin.

15 This All-Pro played in Madison Square Garden and Yankee Stadium in the same year.

16 This Cowboy played baseball in college for the Ohio State Buckeyes before signing as a free agent with the Cowboys.

17 In 1973, Bob Hayes won 15 of 16 special 40-yard match races on a professional track circuit. Who was the one runner who beat him?

18 What were Mel Renfro's track specialties in college?

19 The Cowboys had Calvin Hill rated as a prospect at two other positions. What were they?

26 He switched careers at 26 and is one of the Cowboys' most popular players ever.

27 This "unsung hero" won praise from Tom Landry for his dedication and versatility: He started at three different positions in three Super Bowls.

28 During 1967 and '68, one Cowboy played professionally in Dallas, Oklahoma City and New Orleans.

29 This Cowboy had a master's degree in theology and was an ordained Baptist minister.

30 His Elvis Presley imitations were always in demand at dinner during summer camp.

DALLAS COWBOYS TRIVIA 40 CHALLENGE CONTEST!

Chuck Howley was a five-sport letterman at West Virginia. Other than football and track, in what sports did Howley earn letters?

A. Basketball, baseball, and wrestling. **B.** Basketball, swimming, and wrestling. **C.** Swimming, wrestling, and gymnastics. **D.** Basketball, swimming, and baseball.

---

20 This All-Pro went through position changes with the Cowboys before he found a home (he was both a quarterback and receiver at Clemson).

21 This member of the Dallas Cowboys staff was once a member of the Brooklyn Dodgers baseball organization.

22 This Cowboy once held the United States high school hurdles record with a 13.6. As a collegian he ran a 13.3 and became an NCAA champion. Who was he?

23 In what division did the Cowboys play when the NFL split into four groups in 1967?

24 Where is Tom Landry Stadium?

25 Who is the only former Austin American-Statesman sports writer associated with the Cowboys?

31 He was listed as the backup punter to Danny White before Efren Herrera was moved into the role.

32 When did Bob Hayes win the 100-meter dash in the Olympics?

33 How many Olympic gold medals did Bob Hayes win?

34 This popular Cowboy has become well-known for his prowess on the racquetball courts.

35 This member of the Dallas staff didn't win a gold medal, didn't run a race or throw a javelin ... but he was associated with the 1980 U.S. Olympic team. Who is he?

36 Known more for his defensive work, as a rookie he had a 21-yard pass reception and two kickoff returns (in 1975).

37 This player is often listed as the No. 2 punter. In 1981, he had two punts, averaging 31 yards.

38 As a baseball prospect, he was drafted by four teams — the Houston Astros, Cleveland Indians, New York Mets and Oakland A's.

Cornell Green

39 Billy Cannon Jr. came from a football background but could have chosen professional baseball instead of pro football. Name the two teams, one in each of the two major leagues, that drafted him.

40 What did Wade Manning have in common with Cornell Green and Pete Gent?

41 He was the first draftee by the Dallas Cowboys in the supplemental draft of United States Football League players.

42 What other sports did Roger Staubach play at Navy?

43 This defensive lineman switched positions after volunteering to stay after practice and snap for Roger Staubach and Craig Morton. Who was he?

44 What position did Mike Connelly switch to after four years at center?

45 He was once a high school All-American in New York in lacrosse.

46 He started at cornerback for Missouri ... before being moved to wide receiver ... before being switched back to cornerback by the Cowboys.

47 He attended Holy Cross before transferring to Santa Clara.

48 He started his career at Iowa but transferred to Kentucky State — and he started as a receiver before moving to defense.

49 Who was the former Cowboy punter who tried a comeback with the Cardinals, six years after leaving Dallas?

50 He moved to defensive end when Bob Lilly went to tackle.

DALLAS COWBOYS TRIVIA **41** **CHALLENGE CONTEST!**

Who was the first Cowboy starting quarterback to turn down an offer to play pro baseball?

A. Danny White.   **B.** Craig Morton.   **C.** Gary Hogeboom.   **D.** Roger Staubach.

DALLAS COWBOYS TRIVIA **42** CHALLENGE CONTEST!

This player wasn't normally known for his speed but became known for his play against the rival Washington Redskins. He scored four touchdowns against them without gaining a single yard from scrimmage. Who is he?

A. Bob Lilly. **B.** Larry Cole. **C.** Randy White. **D.** Thomas Henderson.

51 This Cowboy was the NFL's Rookie of the Year in 1961, with another team. Who was he and what team did he play for then?

52 He left Dallas for Philadelphia as a free agent, but instead retired because of nagging injuries.

53 Who moved into Bob Lilly's spot when No. 74 retired?

54 What position did Dave Edwards try before settling in at linebacker for the Cowboys?

(I'D RATHER SWITCH — ANSWERS)

Mike Gaechter has the last word — this time.

1 Running back. Renfro already had been converted to defensive back.

2 Portland, Oregon.

3 Pete Gent.

4 Mike Gaechter.

5 Defensive end.

6 Linebacker.

7 Craig Morton.

8 Bucko Kilroy.

9 New Orleans.

10 He's in a passing pose.

11 Dan Reeves.

12 Mike Ditka.

13 Margene Adkins.

14 Charlie Waters.

15 Cornell Green.

16 Wade Manning.

17 Cliff Branch.

18 The sprints, the high hurdles, and the long jump.

19 Tight end and linebacker.

20 Charlie Waters.

21 Tom (Buck) Buchanan.

22 Richmond Flowers.

23 The Capitol Division.

24 Mission, Texas.

25 Tex Schramm.

26 Roger Staubach.

27 Larry Cole.

28 Ron Widby punted for the Cowboys and a minor-league professional team in Oklahoma City. He also played professional basketball for New Orleans in the ABA.

29 Dave Simmons.

30 Bob Breunig.

31 D.D. Lewis.

32 In 1964.

33 Two.

34 Rafael Septien.

35 Trainer Don Cochren.

36 Bob Breunig.

37 Rafael Septien.

38 Danny White.

39 The New York Yankees and Los Angeles Dodgers.

40 None of them played college football.

41 Todd Fowler.

42 Basketball and baseball.

43 John Fitzgerald.

44 Offensive guard.

45 Tom Rafferty.

46 Ron Fellows.

47 Doug Cosbie.

48 Rod Hill.

49 Marv Bateman.

50 Larry Stephens.

51 Mike Ditka, Chicago.

52 Rayfield Wright.

53 Larry Cole.

54 Offensive end.

Danny White surveys the line.

Craig Morton prepares to unleash a bomb.

Charlie Waters bears down on quarterback Don Strock.

DROP BACK 10 AND PUNT

The kicking game is an important part of every team in the National Football League, and the Cowboys are no exception. From the early years of inconsistency to the days of All-Pro Rafael Septien, the Cowboys have showcased the not-so-great along with the great. Of course, the phrase "drop back 10 and punt" can also be used to refer to the lighter side of football.

Q

1 His fumble of a punt led to the only score for the Dallas Texans in the first regular-season professional football game in Dallas.

2 In 1962, the Cowboys completed a 99-yard touchdown pass against Pittsburgh — but ended up losing points on the play. What happened?

3 Had the 99-yard play been allowed, who would have gone into the record books for the Cowboys?

4 He managed 15 points as a kicker to set the scoring record for the College All-Stars in a 35-19 victory over Detroit in the late 1950s.

5 Who had a PAT blocked in Super Bowl V?

6 This former Kick Karavan product came out of retirement in 1974 to join the Cowboys.

7 What prompted Clint Longley's departure to San Diego?

8 Who fumbled at the Baltimore Colts' two-yard line on a play that could have given the Cowboys a 20-7 lead in Super Bowl V?

9 What happened to Mitch Hoopes' first fourth-quarter punt in Super Bowl X?

10 What game was described by some members of the media as the "Blunder Bowl"?

11 In the 1972 NFC Championship game, what record did Washington's Curt Knight set?

12 What was the largest margin of loss by the Cowboys?

13 During a numbing defeat on national television, this player was seen waving a hanky during the telecast. Shortly

Andy Cvercko

DALLAS COWBOYS TRIVIA **43** CHALLENGE CONTEST!

How many interceptions were there in Super Bowl V?

A. None. **B.** Two. **C.** Five. **D.** Six.

thereafter his career took a dive. Who was he?

14 This player was the victim of the "alarm clock" incident.

15 Which official threw the flag on the key interference call in Super Bowl XIII?

16. In the NFL pool draft, who was the only kicker selected by the fledgling Cowboys?

21 Danny Villanueva handled the kicking duties for the Cowboys in 1966. After the search for a kicker was organized in 1967, who was the No. 1 kicker in the fall of 1967?

22 Who were the only two players to survive the cut after being signed by the kicking expedition in 1967?

23 Who replaced Mike Clark as the Cowboys' kicker in 1971?

DALLAS COWBOYS TRIVIA **44** CHALLENGE CONTEST!

Who was the Cowboys' regular punter in 1960?

A. Eddie LeBaron. **B.** Sam Baker. **C.** Danny Villanueva. **D.** Dave Sherer.

17 Who was the Cowboys' first foreign-born kicker?

18 What was the name of the Cowboys' committee that began a search for a new kicker in 1967?

19 Which former professional kicker organized the Cowboys' search for a kicker in '67?

20 Why was the search begun?

24 He led the nation in punt returns as a junior at Brigham Young University.

25 What was the significance of Toni Fritsch's first PAT attempt in 1975?

26 This player was presented with a yellow crash helmet with a light and siren so that Golden Richards "would know when he's coming my way."

27 Did Roger Staubach ever catch a pass for the Cowboys?

DALLAS COWBOYS TRIVIA **45** CHALLENGE CONTEST!

Who kicked the winning field goal in the Cowboys' first regular-season victory?

A. Sam Baker. **B.** Mike Clark. **C.** Danny Villanueva. **D.** Allen Green.

DALLAS COWBOYS TRIVIA **46** **CHALLENGE CONTEST!**

Who was the first Cowboy to kick a field goal?

A. Sam Baker.   **B.** Billy Lothridge.   **C.** Fred Cone.   **D.** L.G. Dupre.

---

28 These two Cowboys returned field-goal attempts for 60-yard touchdowns in 1965.

29 During the Cowboys' first five seasons, which two punters had 75-yard kicks?

30 He shared the NFL scoring lead in 1957.

31 He subbed for Billy Lothridge as the Cowboys' kicker during the final two games of 1964.

(DROP BACK 10 AND PUNT — ANSWERS)

A

1 Tom Landry, in 1952.

2 Andy Cvercko was flagged for holding on the play — in the end zone — and Pittsburgh was awarded a safety.

3 Eddie LeBaron was the quarterback; Frank Clarke the receiver.

4 Bobby Joe Conrad, who played one year as a wide receiver.

5 Baltimore's Jim O'Brien — who later kicked the winning field goal.

6 Mac Percival.

7 His fights with Roger Staubach.

8 Duane Thomas.

9 The Steelers blocked it out of the end zone for a safety.

10 Super Bowl V — because of the number of mistakes made in the game.

11 Knight kicked the most field goals in an NFC Championship contest, four.

12 Chicago beat Dallas, 44-0, in 1985. Prior to that, Dallas twice lost by 41 points. In 1960, Cleveland beat the Cowboys, 48-7, and in 1970 the Min-

Rafael Septien with his mentor, Ben Agajanian.

DALLAS COWBOYS TRIVIA **47** CHALLENGE CONTEST!

In 1960, who was the Cowboys player who handled the backup chores, punting three times?

A. Billy Lothridge. **B.** Eddie LeBaron. **C.** Don Perkins. **D.** Fred Cone.

nesota Vikings beat them by a 54-13 margin. Of course, after the Vikings beat the Cowboys, Dallas went on to its first Super Bowl appearance.

13 Thomas (Hollywood) Henderson.

14 A malfunctioning alarm clock was blamed for Tony Dorsett being late to a workout. Dorsett was benched for a short time after the incident.

15 Fred Swearingen.

16 Dave Sherer.

17 Toni Fritsch.

18 The Kick Karavan.

19 Ben Agajanian.

20 The Cowboys were unhappy with the performance of kicker Danny Villanueva during the 1966 season.

21 Danny Villanueva.

22 Mac Percival and Harold Deters.

23 Tony Fritsch.

24 Golden Richards.

25 The kick was no good — after Fritsch had kicked 81 in a row during his first three seasons.

26 Cliff Harris.

27 Yes, one for a loss of 13 yards.

28 Obert Logan and Mike Gaechter.

29 Sam Baker (in 1962) and Billy Lothridge (in '64).

30 Kicker Sam Baker. Later, he led the Cowboys in scoring two times.

31 Tight end Lee Folkins.

PASSING FANCY

Would you believe that Roger Staubach doesn't have one of the top 10 single-game passing efforts in Dallas Cowboys history?

In 1984, Gary Hogeboom's 343-yard passing effort against the Los Angeles Rams was the 10th best in Cowboy history — and moved Staubach out of the top 10 standings. Two entries in 1985 bumped that effort off the list.

Following are the 10 best single-game passing marks in Dallas history:

460 yards — Don Meredith at San Francisco, Nov. 10, 1963 (30 of 48).
406 yards — Don Meredith at Washington, Nov. 13, 1966 (21 of 29).
394 yards — Don Meredith at Philadelphia, Nov. 6, 1966 (14 of 24).
389 yards — Gary Hogeboom at San Francisco, Dec. 22, 1985 (28 of 49).
377 yards — Danny White vs. Tampa Bay, Oct. 9, 1983 (29 of 44).
362 yards — Danny White vs. Atlanta, Oct. 27, 1985 (27 of 47).
358 yards — Don Meredith vs. N.Y. Giants, Sept. 18, 1966 (14 of 24).
354 yards — Danny White vs. Miami, Oct. 25, 1981 (22 of 32).
349 yards — Craig Morton vs. Houston, Dec. 20, 1970 (13 of 17).
347 yards — Danny White vs. Pittsburgh, Sept. 13, 1982 (25 of 36).

THE ENVELOPE, PLEASE

From Heisman trophy winners to Hall of Famers, the Dallas Cowboys have garnered their share of honors. Many Cowboys have been recognized for their prowess on the field . . . and several have also been honored for work in other fields.

Q

Bob Lilly gets a turn as a ball-carrier.

1 Who was the first Cowboys quarterback to finish in the top 10 voting for the Heisman trophy?

2 This defensive back was selected to play in the Pro Bowl 10 times.

3 He was selected to play in 11 Pro Bowls for the Cowboys.

4 What was the halftime feature in the Cowboys' home game against the Philadelphia Eagles in 1975?

5 What was Randy White's biggest present on his 25th birthday?

6 This future Cowboy was named the top lineman in the Pro Bowl in 1957.

7 What happened at halftime in 197 when the Cowboys played the New York Giants?

| DALLAS COWBOYS TRIVIA | **48** | CHALLENGE CONTEST! |

How many times have the Cowboys won the Lombardi Trophy?

A. Five.   **B.** None.   **C.** Two.   **D.** Three

88

DALLAS COWBOYS TRIVIA **49** CHALLENGE CONTEST!

He was named the outstanding back in the 1971 Pro Bowl.

A. Calvin Hill. **B.** Charlie Waters. **C.** Duane Thomas. **D.** Mel Renfro.

---

8 Which Cowboy was once voted the top track and field performer in high school in the United States?

9 What did Haggar call its weekly award for the Cowboys?

10 What did Ken's Man Shop present to the Cowboys after each game?

11 The year Tony Dorsett won the Heisman trophy, what future Cowboy won the Maxwell Award as College Player of the Year?

15 From 1974 through '79, Roger Staubach won the annual Oak Farms Dairies Favorite Cowboy award five times. Who interrupted his streak in 1978?

16 What year did Chuck Howley enter the Ring of Honor?

17 What year did Roger Staubach enter the Ring of Honor?

18 Which two players were making their 10th Pro Bowl appearances following

---

DALLAS COWBOYS TRIVIA **50** CHALLENGE CONTEST!

Who was the other Cowboy who went into the Pro Football Hall of Fame the same year as Bob Lilly?

A. Don Meredith. **B.** Lance Alworth. **C.** Herb Adderley. **D.** Don Perkins.

---

12 These two future Cowboys were members of the 1960 Kodak All-American team.

13 He was a member of the same team and a Cowboys draft pick — but never played for the Cowboys.

14 This Cowboy was named Lone Star Conference Defensive Player of the Decade for the 1970s.

the 1973 season?

19 Who was the first offensive lineman to win the annual Oak Farms Dairies Favorite Cowboy contest?

20 How many times was Charlie Waters voted the Oak Farms Dairies Favorite Cowboy for the season?

21 Which Cowboy draft pick joined Lee Roy Jordan on the College All-Star

---

DALLAS COWBOYS TRIVIA **51** CHALLENGE CONTEST!

Who was named the East's outstanding lineman in the 1970 Pro Bowl?

A. George Andrie. **B.** Bob Lilly. **C.** Jethro Pugh. **D.** Willie Townes.

team against the Packers in 1963?

22 What was the first year Tony Dorsett was named All-Pro?

23 Only two Cowboys were named All-Pro each of their first two years with Dallas. Name them.

24 Who were the only two Cowboys named All-Pro in 1975?

25 He was an All-Pro in 1954.

26 He won the Walter Camp Memorial Award in 1963 as a collegian.

27 In 1971, this Cowboy was named NFL Player of the Year by "The Sporting News."

28 He was named to two positions on All-NFL teams in 1966.

29 Who was named the 1971 Players Association Most Valuable Player?

30 What does Roger Staubach have in common with Doak Walker, Vic Janowicz, Archie Griffin, and Billy Sims?

31 Tony Dorsett said he would place this award next to his Heisman in his trophy case.

32 He was named NFL Rookie of the Year, Oak Farms Dairies Favorite Cowboy and Cowboys Bachelor of the Year, all in one season.

33 What did Chuck Howley win in Super Bowl V?

34 What NFL Alumni Association award did Bill Bates win in 1983?

35 He was named the Outstanding Defensive Player of the 1983 Fiesta Bowl.

36 In 1979, he was named by teens in a Gallup Survey as their favorite sports personality.

37 Who was the second choice in the survey?

38 Who was the Cowboys' first winner of the NFL Man of the Year Award?

39 Who was the Cowboys' first two-time

Ready, set, launch. Roger Staubach gets ready to zip another rocket.

winner of the NFL Man of the Year Award?

40 Who took over sponsorship of the NFL Man of the Year Award in 1980?

41 Who was voted the Cowboys' NFL Man of the Year in 1980?

42 Who was the first defensive player to be named the Cowboys' NFL Man of the Year?

43 This tight end was named Cowboys NFL Man of the Year in 1982.

44 What year did Danny White first win

90

the Cowboys' NFL Man of the Year Award?

45 What year did the NFL Man of the Year Award begin?

46 He was named Notre Dame's Offensive Most Valuable Player for 1981.

47 Three Cowboys were named to the Pro Bowl for the first time in 1981. One was a rookie, one was in his fifth year, and one was a seven-year veteran. Name them.

48 This Pennsylvania high school player was named All-State and All-American for defense and offense as a junior.

49 Who was the first freshman in 29 years to earn a place as a College All-American (in 1973)?

50 Who was the Most Valuable Player in Super Bowl X, Dallas' third Super Bowl appearance?

51 Who were the first Heisman trophy winners to enter the Pro Football Hall of Fame?

52 Who was named Associated Press Defensive Player of the Year in 1977?

53 Who received the same award from United Press International in 1978?

54 Who was the first Cowboy to win a Seagram Seven Crowns award?

55 Who were the opposing quarterbacks on hand for presentation of the Dallas All-Sports Association Distinguished Service Award in 1980?

56 Who won the 1978 Brian Piccolo YMCA Humanitarian Award?

57 He was named Most Valuable Player by his Detroit Lions teammates in 1952.

Speed merchant Tony Dorsett weaves another masterpiece.

58 He was the Southwest Conference Sophomore of the Year in 1953.

59 Which two Cowboys were selected to play for the College All-Stars in 1961?

60 Which five Cowboys were named to

DALLAS COWBOYS TRIVIA **52** **CHALLENGE CONTEST!**

Who was the first Pitt player to win the Heisman?

A. Mike Ditka. **B.** Tony Dorsett. **C.** Roger Staubach. **D.** Ernie Stautner.

*Billy Joe DuPree rides into
shape once again.*

the NFL's All-Rookie team in 1961?

61 In 1961, who did the "Dallas Times Herald" list as its outstanding Southwest Conference lineman in its poll of conference players?

62 He was named United Press International Back of the Week four times in 1958.

63 These three players were named to the 1962 NFL All-Rookie team.

64 Who won the Maxwell Award in 1956?

65 Who won the Walter Camp Award in 1956?

66 Who was the only Cowboy named to the 1963 NFL All-Rookie team?

67 Who was named Most Valuable Player in the Blue-Gray Game in 1977?

68 Who were the Cowboys' All-Rookie selections in 1964?

69 Who were the two picks in 1965?

70 Who was second to Gale Sayers in Rookie of the Year voting in 1965?

71 Who was the only Cowboy named to the All-Rookie team in 1966?

72 Who was the Southeast Conference's Player of the Year for 1967?

73 In 1980, he was named by New York sportswriters to the New York High School All-Decade Team as a linebacker.

74 What honor did Tex Schramm originate to honor players instead of retiring their jersey numbers?

75 Who was named the Custom Tailors' Guild of New York's Best Dressed Man in Sports in 1981?

76 Which Cowboy was named to the 1970's All-Decade Team by the Pro Football Hall of Fame?

77 Which future Cowboy was a finalist for the Lombardi Award in 1980?

78 What was the name of the "Pro Football Weekly" award that Rafael Septien received following the 1981 season?

79 He was named the "Football News" National Football Conference Player of the Year for 1980.

80 How many times did Roger Staubach win the weekly Oak Farms Dairies Favorite Cowboy award?

81 Who was the first player to win the weekly award five times in a single season?

82 He was the NFL Man of the Year in 1980, and joined the Cowboys in 1984.

83 In which four seasons did the

Cowboys have nine players named to the Pro Bowl?

84 Name the only player selected to the Pro Bowl for the latter two years.

85 What year did the Cowboys have two All-Pro guards?

86 That same year, Dallas had another offensive lineman named All-Pro. Who was he?

87 Who was the first individual member of the Cowboys to win the Dallas All-Sports Association's Field Scovell Award?

88 Who won the Scovell award in 1975?

89 What year did Randy White claim the Field Scovell Award?

90 And who was named winner the following year?

91 This player was voted the Outstanding Lineman at Tennessee by his teammates in 1960 — and compared to Bob Lilly by Tom Landry.

92 What did the player have in common with Lilly?

93 He was the Offensive Player of the Year in the Pacific Coast Athletic Conference in 1976.

94 He was inducted into the NAIA Hall of Fame in 1977.

95 That same year, this player was named Pro Athlete of the Year by the South Carolina Athletic Hall of Fame.

(THE ENVELOPE, PLEASE — ANSWERS)

Randy White dances into the Cardinal backfield.

1 Eddie LeBaron was sixth in the voting in 1949.

2 Mel Renfro.

3 Bob Lilly.

4 Bob Lilly's enshrinement in the Ring of Honor.

5 He was named co-MVP in Super Bowl XII.

6 Ernie Stautner.

7 Don Perkins and Don Meredith were inducted into the Ring of Honor.

8 Mel Renfro.

9 The Haggar Headhunter Award for specialty teams play.

10 The Big Play Award.

11 Tony Dorsett.

12 Bob Lilly and Mike Ditka.

13 E.J. Holub.

14 Harvey Martin.

15 Charlie Waters.

16 In 1977.

17 In 1983.

18 Bob Lilly and Mel Renfro. Lilly was named for the 11th time, but had missed once with an injury.

19 Jim Cooper.

20 Twice.

21 Sonny Gibbs.

22 The 1981 season.

23 Mel Renfro and Everson Walls.

24 Rayfield Wright and Cliff Harris.

25 Tom Landry.

26 Roger Staubach.

27 Roger Staubach.

28 Bob Hayes (split end on the AP and UPI teams and flanker on the NEA — a matter of semantics).

29 Roger Staubach.

30 Each won the Heisman trophy his junior year.

31 The Field Scovell Award from the Dallas All-Sports Association in 1981.

32 Calvin Hill.

33 A Dodge Charger for being named Super Bowl Most Valuable Player.

34 Special Teams Player of the Year.

35 Jim Jeffcoat.

36 Roger Staubach.

37 Tony Dorsett.

38 Calvin Hill.

39 Roger Staubach.

40 Miller Brewing Company.

41 Drew Pearson.

42 D.D. Lewis.

43 Billy Joe DuPree.

44 In 1983.

45 In 1970. It was discontinued from 1977 through '79 and resumed in 1980.

46 Phil Pozderac.

47 In order: Everson Walls, Rafael Septien, and Ed (Too Tall) Jones.

48 Tony Dorsett.

49 Tony Dorsett.

50 Pittsburgh's Lynn Swann.

51 Roger Staubach and O.J. Simpson.

52 Harvey Martin.

53 Randy White.

54 Rayfield Wright.

55 Terry Bradshaw presented the award to Roger Staubach.

56 Roger Staubach.

57 Jim Doran.

58 Don McIlhenny.

59 Bob Lilly and Glynn Gregory.

60 Bob Lilly, Don Perkins, Ken Frost, Warren Livingston, and Amos Marsh.

61 Don Talbert.

62 Don Meredith.

63 Mike Gaechter, George Andrie, and Guy Reese.

64 Tommy McDonald.

65 Jerry Tubbs.

66 Lee Roy Jordan.

67 Todd Christensen.

68 Jake Kupp and Mel Renfro.

69 Bob Hayes and Ralph Neely.

70 Bob Hayes.

71 Willie Townes.

72 D.D. Lewis.

73 Jay Saldi.

74 The Ring of Honor.

75 Tony Dorsett.

76 Drew Pearson.

77 Howard Richards.

78 The Golden Toe Award.

Rayfield Wright (left) leads the way for Robert Newhouse.

79 Randy White.

80 Fifteen.

81 Danny White (in 1981).

82 Harold Carmichael.

83 In 1966, 1967, 1971, and 1978.

84 Roger Staubach was selected in 1971 and '78.

85 In 1972 (Blaine Nye and John Niland).

86 Rayfield Wright.

87 Bob Lilly in 1971.

88 Roger Staubach.

89 In 1980.

90 Tony Dorsett.

91 Ken Frost.

92 Both were defensive linemen, but Frost played just two years and wasn't a regular.

93 Steve DeBerg.

94 Cliff Harris.

95 Charlie Waters.

The Beautiful Harvey Martin, 1977's defensive gem.

YOU CAN QUOTE ME

With a little help from the media, the Dallas Cowboys have had their say - sometimes too much, it would seem.

Tradition has it that almost every season, a quote winds up on an opposing team's bulletin board as a reminder, or as fodder to help fuel a rivalry. Tom Landry, like every other head coach, has been known to frown — out loud - after some quotes appeared in print before a big game.

This time, Tom Landry had to answer to Don Meredith.

1 Following Dallas' first Super Bowl triumph, which Cowboy stormed into the locker room in the midst of the celebration yelling, "I want to be interviewed"?

2 Who said, in referring to the Super Bowl, "If this is the ultimate game, why are they playing it again next year"?

3 Many times a player decides to keep his quotes out of the newspapers in order to avoid controversy and to keep from being misquoted. This player not only refused to talk to the media, he also refused to talk to almost anyone on the team or coaching staff — except when absolutely necessary.

4 Was he serious? Who said, "You never know when you'll be surrounded by Redskins"?

5 Who was sportswriter Bob St. John referring to when he wrote, "His idea of breaking training is putting whipped cream on his pie"?

6 Who said, "I had a dream that a long field goal was going to win the Super Bowl"?

7 Pete Gent said, "Don't bother reading it kid. Everybody gets killed in the end." What was he talking about?

8 Who said, "To us, there is no success unless we win it all"?

9 "Until I'm able to put a Super Bowl ring on everyone's finger, there's no way I can be satisfied," said this Cowboy. Who was speaking?

10 What was Larry Cole's excuse when a reporter pointed out that it had been almost 10 years between his third and fourth professional touchdowns?

11 "Tackling him is like tackling a shot put." Who was Dave Edwards talking about?

12 Who said, "The Cowboys are the most overrated, overhyped team in professional football"?

13 What was Robert Newhouse's answer

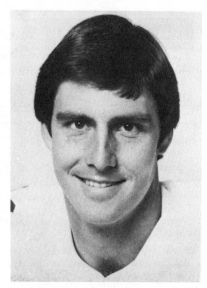

Danny White

to critics who asked if he thought his height would be a disadvantage?

14 Whom did Bob Lilly credit with "having more of a positive influence on my life than anybody" when he was inducted into the Pro Football Hall of Fame?

15 What was Tex Schramm's reaction to Duane Thomas' charge that he was "sick, demented, and completely dishonest"?

16 Before Super Bowl VI, he said, "What does closeness mean ... the Saint players are closely knit and they lose a lot." Who was the spokesman?

17 NFL great Jim Brown called this Cowboy "the epitome of an artist." Who was he talking about?

18 What was Tom Landry referring to when he said, "I think that title gave us a lot more trouble than it was worth"?

19 Who said, "You could make more money investing in government bonds, but football is more fun"?

DALLAS COWBOYS TRIVIA **53** **CHALLENGE CONTEST!**

This Cowboy said, "Rooming with Roger Staubach is like rooming with my father."

A. Drew Pearson. **B.** Craig Morton. **C.** Danny White. **D.** Bob Breunig.

---

20 What did Washington's Diron Talbert say about Roger Staubach that helped fuel the two players' feud?

21 Which Cowboy said of the name-calling with the Redskins on Thanksgiving Day, "I told them they were turkeys and they said I was a hot dog"?

22 Who said the best way to prepare for Dallas was "just pretend the Cowboys are Iranians"?

23 Who said, "They've built me up as the guy who's going to change the Dallas Cowboys"?

24 Who was Dan Reeves talking about when he said, "He was just a blur against the linebackers"?

25 Who said of Tony Dorsett, "When his career is over, there probably won't be many NFL records that won't have his name on them"?

26 During a Dallas comeback against Washington, Brad Sham declared, "If they cash this thing in, we're running him for Congress." Who was he talking about?

27 Steve Wilson once muffed a kick in the end zone and didn't know he could have downed it for a touchback rather than run it out and be tackled at the four. What was his comment about the play?

28 Tom Landry called him "another Bob Hayes" after he clocked a 4.5 in the 40 in Levis. Who was he referring to?

29 Coach Landry said of this No. 3, 1973 draft pick, "If a player like this hits, you've got one who will help you for 10

years." Who was he talking about?

30 Of this No. 7, 1973 draft choice, Tom Landry said, "He has so much poten

Robert Newhouse

tial that if he doesn't come on to be a great one, I'll be surprised." Who was he talking about this time?

31 This Zero Club member, when asked why he played professional football, answered, "Because playing rugby would have required moving to England." Who was he?

DALLAS COWBOYS TRIVIA **54** **CHALLENGE CONTEST!**

On October 16, 1978, newscaster Paul Harvey reported he had been traded to Chicago for Bob Avellini and Robin Earl. Who was the subject of the report?

A. Tony Dorsett. **B.** Randy White. **C.** Danny White. **D.** Glenn Carano.

(YOU CAN QUOTE ME — ANSWERS)

1 Bob Lilly.

2 Duane Thomas.

3 You guessed it — again — Duane Thomas.

4 Tom Landry, in an American Express commercial.

5 Roger Staubach.

6 Jim O'Brien, whose 32-yard field goal beat the Cowboys in Super Bowl V.

7 The Cowboys' playbook.

8 Tex Schramm.

9 Danny White.

10 Cole said anyone could have an off decade.

11 Robert Newhouse.

12 Howard Cosell.

13 Newhouse said, "I'm not going to grow an inch but maybe I can play a little bigger than I am."

14 Tom Landry.

15 Schramm said, "That's not bad. He got two out of three."

16 Calvin Hill.

17 Tony Dorsett.

18 The "America's Team" label that stuck with the Cowboys.

19 Clint Murchison.

20 Talbert said he was surprised Dallas started Staubach over Craig Morton in the 1972 NFC title game against the Redskins.

21 Thomas (Hollywood) Henderson.

22 Diron Talbert, who else?

23 Tony Dorsett.

24 Again, Tony Dorsett.

25 O.J. Simpson.

26 The master of the comeback — Roger Staubach.

27 "I didn't know the rule and I didn't have time to look it up."

28 Margene Adkins, who didn't quite live up to that billing in his two years with the Cowboys.

29 Harvey Martin, who played 11 seasons for the Cowboys.

30 Rodrigo Barnes, who was with the team only two seasons.

31 Blaine Nye.

TURKEY DAY

The Cowboys have gained plenty of exposure from the tradition they began i
the 1960s by playing on Thanksgiving Day. Fans have grown accustomed t
seeing Dallas play while putting away the turkey and trimmings. And th
Cowboys have enjoyed the tradition, too, with numerous victories.

Roger Staubach eludes the Redskin pursuit.

Q

1 Who replaced Roger Staubach on Thanksgiving Day 1974, when Staubach was knocked out of the game?

2 What year did the Cowboys first play a game on Thanksgiving Day?

3 Who was the opponent and what was the score in Dallas' first Thanksgiving Day game?

4 How many years did Dallas play a Thanksgiving Day game before losing for the first time?

5 Which team broke Dallas' first Thanksgiving Day winning streak?

6 The Cowboys have played only fiv times against AFC teams o Thanksgiving Day. Name the teams.

7 What is the Cowboys' record again those AFC teams on Thanksgivi Day?

8 Which was the first team to bea Dallas on Thanksgiving Day?

9 What years did the Cowboys not pla on Thanksgiving Day after the trad tion began?

10 Who won in Roger Staubach's la Thanksgiving Day game?

11 How many times have the Cowbo

DALLAS COWBOYS TRIVIA **55** CHALLENGE CONTEST!

Who were the first three teams to beat the Cowboys in Thanksgiving Day games?

A. Miami, San Francisco, and Cleveland. **B.** San Francisco, Houston, and Los Angeles. **C.** Miami, San Francisco, and Houston. **D.** Washington, St. Louis, and San Francisco.

played Washington on Thanksgiving Day?

12 Which team has Dallas played the most on Thanksgiving Day?

13 How many times have the Redskins beaten the Cowboys on Thanksgiving Day?

14 How many times has Dallas played on the road on Thanksgiving Day?

15 Who was the victim when the Cowboys scored 51 points on Thanksgiving Day in 1980?

16 Which team did the Cowboys hold to a single field goal on Thanksgiving Day in 1970?

17 How many times on Thanksgiving Day have the Cowboys won by a single point?

18 Only once has the winner of a Dallas Thanksgiving Day game scored just 10 points. What was the score and who was the opponent?

19 Who was the Cowboys' opponent on Thanksgiving Day when the teams combined for a total of 67 points?

20 What year did a Thanksgiving Day game end in a tie — and who was the opponent?

21 How many overtime games has Dallas played on Thanksgiving Day?

22 This Dallas running back zipped 59 yards on one play and ran for a game-high 122 yards and two touchdowns against the Redskins in the 1978 Thanksgiving Day game.

23 This Cowboy had 51 yards — on only four carries — and scored on a 39-yard touchdown against Washington in the same game.

24 In the 1983 Thanksgiving Day game, this player ran for 102 yards and scored twice (including once on a 55-yard jaunt).

25 Besides the 1981 game, one other Thanksgiving Day matchup resulted in only 19 points. Who did Dallas beat in that one?

26 In their game against the Oilers on Thanksgiving Day 1979, the Cowboys were penalized for having 12 men on the field. Who was the 12th man — and what did the play mean to the game?

DALLAS COWBOYS TRIVIA **56** CHALLENGE CONTEST!

Like Clint Longley before him, this quarterback got his first chance to play under pressure in a Thanksgiving Day game. Who was he?

A. Roger Staubach. **B.** Steve Pelluer. **C.** Glenn Carano. **D.** Brad Wright.

(TURKEY DAY — ANSWERS)

A 1 Clint Longley.

2 In 1966.

3 The Cleveland Browns; Dallas won the game, 26-14.

4 Dallas was unbeaten in its first six; the Cowboys won five and tied one.

5 San Francisco broke the winning streak — and also the unbeaten streak.

6 Miami (1973), Houston (1979), Seattle (1980), Cleveland (1982), and New England (1984). When Dallas played Cleveland in 1966, the Browns were still in the NFL — not in the AFC.

7 Dallas beat all but Miami and Houston.

8 San Francisco, 31-10, in 1972.

9 In 1975 and 1977.

10 Houston won, 30-24.

11 Three.

12 St. Louis (four times).

13 None.

14 None.

15 Seattle; Dallas won, 51-7.

16 Green Bay in 1970.

17 Twice, in 1974 against Washington and in 1981 against Chicago.

18 Dallas won, 10-9, over Chicago.

19 The St. Louis Cardinals; Dallas won the game, 46-21.

20 The year was 1969. Dallas and San Francisco tied, 24-24.

21 None.

22 Scott Laidlaw.

23 Larry Brinson.

24 Tony Dorsett.

25 Green Bay (in 1970) by a 16-3 score.

26 Dave Stalls was the 12th man. Houston was given a second chance on a play and went on to win, 30-24.

Tony Dorsett gets started on one of his standard, everyday long gainers.

Clint Longley — the kid who made good on his Thanksgiving Day chance.

IT'S SHOWTIME

One of the hardest things for a professional athlete is to make the transition from the life of games to the game of life. But many Cowboys have moved on to other fields of entertainment with ease. Entertainers also have played parts in the history of the team — beginning with the first regular-season game in 1960.

Q

1 Which cowboy put on a pre-game show before the first Dallas game in the inaugural season?

2 Which three teams had players suited up for Super Bowl X?

3 Super Bowl X provided the backdrop for a movie. What was it?

5 What wrinkle did Thomas (Hollywood) Henderson add to the spike in 1977?

6 What was the name of Harvey Martin's radio show on KFJZ?

7 Which two Cowboys appeared in the movie version of Dan Jenkins' novel "Semi-Tough"?

DALLAS COWBOYS TRIVIA **57** **CHALLENGE CONTEST!**

Who is the regular featured trumpeter who plays the "National Anthem" at Cowboys games?

A. Boots Randolph. **B.** Ace Cannon. **C.** Tommy Loy. **D.** Billy Clampett.

---

4 This junior college drill team was one of the most popular halftime acts at Cowboys games in the 1960s and '70s.

8 These two golden throats were masters of ceremonies at the Cowboys 25th anniversary celebration.

DALLAS COWBOYS TRIVIA **58** **CHALLENGE CONTEST!**

Four Cowboys played bikers in this movie.

A. "Easy Rider." **B.** "Squeezze Play." **C.** "Hell's Angels Forever." **D.** "Born To Lose."

---

9 What was "Shoot For The Stars"?

10 What was "Team On A Tightrope"?

11 What was "Funkin' On The Radio"?

12 What was the flip side of "Funkin' On The Radio"?

13 Who sang "Turn out the lights . . ." to the delight of millions of television viewers?

14 What airline had a plane made up in Cowboys team colors and logo?

15 What former Dallas player won a television Emmy for his performance.

16 Which player had a role in a television movie about a football player from Pittsburgh and the kid who offered him a Coke?

17 Who was the first member of the Cowboys to do a Lite beer commercial?

18 Craig Morton, John Niland, and D.D. Lewis had roles in this horror movie.

19 This Cowboy had parts in three movies and a TV series, plus cut a record.

"Bear," the film about Alabama's Bear Bryant.

24 What year did the Cowboys play in the first nationally televised Monday night game?

25 Which player teamed with Verne Lundquist and Jerry Haynes on the WFAA-TV sports team in the early 1970s?

26 He played the organ and his wife was a singer-dancer-actress, with a role in a Richard Burton movie.

27 This Fort Worth organization provided entertainment at Cowboys games in the 1960s and '70s.

28 What was the year of the Cowboys' first defeat on ABC's "Monday Night Football" telecast?

29 After his retirement from football, this Cowboy took part in television productions and began an acting career. He had several roles in the television series, "Police Story."

30 In a Dallas theater production, this former Cowboy starred in the play,

---

DALLAS COWBOYS TRIVIA **59** **CHALLENGE CONTEST!**

This former player had roles in two movies that dealt with football teams, "North Dallas Forty" and "Heaven Can Wait."

A. Don Meredith.   **B.** D.D. Lewis.   **C.** Lance Rentzel.   **D.** Jim Boecke.

---

20 This TV personality had the longest tenure of radio broadcasters with the Cowboys: 15 years.

21 Who was the play-by-play announcer the year the Cowboys went to their first Super Bowl?

22 This radio announcer from 1965 through '71 later was the TV voice of "World Championship Wrestling" in Dallas.

23 This member of the Cowboys served as a consultant to the producers of

"Damn Yankees."

31 When off the football field, players are often called upon for "hazardous" duty. Five Cowboys were once called on to test their skills on the TV show, "Family Feud." Name the five who participated in the 1980 show.

32 Who were their opponents?

33 What member of the Cowboys' organization used to be a regular on a Sid Caeser TV show?

34 What entertainer was Texie Waterman married to?

35 This Dallas Cowboys group was subject of a pair of made-for-TV movies.

36 He was wired for sound in one of his final games and featured in an NFL Films production, "Big Game America."

37 Why did TV commentator Tom Landry say he switched to picking Miami in Super Bowl XIX — after earlier predicting San Francisco would win?

38 Two Dallas games are in the top 10-rated television programs of all time. What are they?

39 Who, in a television commercial for a bank, declared, "The difference is they have to be nice, but I gotta be mean"?

40 Which Dallas television station did Ron Springs work for during his first off-season in Dallas?

41 What place on the all-time top-10 sports telecasts does Super Bowl XII hold?

42 Which Cowboys game was ranked in the top 10 sports telecasts of 1984?

43 With hat in hand and shirt open, this Cowboy had his own beefcake poster in the late 1970s.

44 What was the Tony Dorsett rumor that Jimmy The Greek was spreading in 1978?

45 He appeared in Jas. K. Wilson ads in Dallas home-game programs in the 1960s and '70s.

46 This 13th-round draft choice in 1973

Don Meredith, pre-ABC.

appeared in the movie, "Save The Tiger."

47 He did guest shots on the PBA Spanish series, "Sonrisas."

48 Who recorded the song, "Dallas Cowboys," in the late 1970s?

49 His single was No. 2 behind a Beatles tune for a few weeks in 1965. Name him and the record.

DALLAS COWBOYS TRIVIA **60** **CHALLENGE CONTEST!**

This entertainer was interviewed during the nationally televised Dallas-Buffalo game in 1976.

A. Olivia Newton-John. **B.** Huey Lewis. **C.** Howard Cosell.
D. John Lennon.

50 What did "Us" magazine list as one of its "Flops of '79"?

51 What was the name of the Dallas Cowboys Cheerleaders' second made-for-TV movie?

52 Besides trainer Don Cochren, who else with a Cowboy connection was on hand to work at the 1980 Winter Olympics?

53 Who cut a pop single about the Cowboys in 1980?

54 What happened to Herb Adderley in the 28-7 victory over the New York Giants in 1971 that promoted Ike Thomas from the taxi squad?

55 What was the first nationally-televised Dallas Cowboys game?

56 This Cowboy draft pick from Texas Tech had a bit part in the movie, "Hud."

57 He appeared in NBC's made-for-TV movie, "Undercover With The KKK."

58 Which team won more money on the special edition of "Family Feud" that featured two Cowboy groups?

59 These two Cowboys appeared in 7-Up commercials in the late 1970s.

60 He finished third in the 1983 "SuperStars" competition.

61 Who appeared on the TV Show, "Different Strokes"?

62 Who did commercials for Skoal smokeless tobacco?

63 Who did the Lipton Tea commercials?

64 Who did commercials for John Deere equipment?

65 Who did commercials for the "Dallas Morning News" when Blackie Sherrod moved from the "Dallas Times Herald"?

66 Who teamed with Joe Theismann in a commercial for sportswear?

67 Who did commercials for Black & Decker?

68 Who did a commercial for Haverty's Furniture?

69 Who were the four Cowboys who appeared in "Squeezze Play"?

DALLAS COWBOYS TRIVIA **61** **CHALLENGE CONTEST!**

In "Dallas Cowboys: The First Twenty-Five Years," which commercial did author Carlton Stowers list as the best ever done by a member of the Cowboys' organization?

A. Tom Landry's American Express commercial. **B.** Ed Jones' Atari commercial. **C.** Billy Joe DuPree's United Way spot. **D.** Roger Staubach's Rolaids commercial.

(IT'S SHOWTIME — ANSWERS)

1 Roy Rogers (and the Sons of the Pioneers).

2 Dallas, Pittsburgh, and Miami. The Dolphins were taking part in the filming of a movie.

3 "Black Sunday."

4 The Tyler Junior College Apache Belles.

5 The crossbar, slam-dunk spike.

Harvey Martin — in a not-so-beautiful pose.

6 "The Beautiful Harvey Martin Show."

7 Ed Jones and Thomas Henderson.

8 Pat Summerall and Frank Gifford.

9 The NFL Films production about the Cowboys' first 25 years.

10 The title of the 1979 Dallas Cowboys highlight film.

11 The name of Ed (Too Tall) Jones' 45-rpm record.

12 "Doin' The Dip."

13 Don Meredith on ABC's "Monday Night Football," whenever the game was out of hand.

14 Braniff.

15 Don Meredith for his work on "Monday Night Football."

16 Harvey Martin in the made-for-TV movie, "Mean Joe Greene and The Pittsburgh Kid."

17 Ernie Stautner.

18 "Horror High."

19 Ed (Too Tall) Jones.

Lance Rentzel, organist and receiver.

20 Verne Lundquist.

21 Bill Mercer.

22 Bill Mercer.

23 Assistant coach Gene Stallings, who was an assistant to Bryant. Stallings also worked with actor Gary Busey, who portrayed Bryant in the movie.

24 In 1968, although ABC didn't begin its Monday night feature until later.

25 Frank Clarke.

26 Lance Rentzel. His wife was Joey Heatherton.

27 The Lions Club Band of Greater Fort Worth.

28 In 1970, the first year for the show.

29 Don Meredith.

30 Harvey Martin.

31 Harvey Martin, Tony Dorsett, Charlie Waters, Larry Cole, and Danny White.

32 The Dallas Cowboys Cheerleaders.

33 Texie Waterman, the Cheerleaders' choreographer.

34 Arte Johnson.

35 The Dallas Cowboys Cheerleaders.

36 Don Meredith.

37 Landry said O.J. Simpson, who was also doing the game for ABC, was a 49ers fan and he (Landry) just wanted to make it interesting.

38 Super Bowl XII and Super Bowl XIII.

39 Harvey Martin.

40 KXAS (Channel 5).

41 Third place.

42 The Dallas-Miami regular-season finale on ABC-TV.

43 Charlie Waters.

44 That Dorsett would be on the trading block at the end of the season.

45 Tom Landry.

46 Colorado kicker Fred Lima.

47 Rafael Septien.

48 Charley Pride.

49 Buddy Dial; the song was "Baby."

50 The boxing career of Ed (Too Tall) Jones.

51 "Dallas Cowboys Cheerleaders II."

52 Don Meredith (working for ABC-TV).

53 The Dallas Cowboys Cheerleaders.

54 In an incident similar to "The Fortune Cookie," Adderley collided with a TV cameraman. Unlike the movie, the player was hurt.

55 A Dec. 11, 1965 game against St. Louis.

56 Denton Fox.

57 Don Meredith.

58 The Cowboys defeated the Cheerleaders, winning $12,000.

59 Tony Dorsett and Thomas (Hollywood) Henderson.

60 Tony Hill.

61 Ed (Too Tall) Jones.

62 Walt Garrison.

63 Don Meredith.

64 Walt Garrison.

65 Drew Pearson (along with several other Dallas sports personalities).

66 Ed (Too Tall) Jones.

67 Bob Lilly.

68 Clint Murchison.

69 Jay Saldi, Drew Pearson, Thomas (Hollywood) Henderson, and Ed (Too Tall) Jones.

Buddy Dial: "Baby, he could catch 'em."

IS THERE A DOCTOR IN THE HOUSE?

Injuries play an important part in professional football. Sometimes the difference between a contender and champion is determined by injuries. Like most teams, the Cowboys have had their share of players hurt in the line of duty.

A headline-maker off the field.

Q 1 Once Randy White became a regular, what finally forced him to miss a game?

2 Which Cowboy suffered a minor injury during Dallas' last offensive series in the "Ice Bowl" that affected his vision on the following critical pass play?

3 What happened to Don Perkins during workouts with the College All-Stars in 1960?

4 A one-time Most Outstanding Prep Player in Oklahoma, this Cowboy's future was cut short by injuries in 1981.

5 Why did the Cowboys return Calvin Hill to the running back position — after considering him at tight end — during his first training camp?

6 Mike Gaechter was forced to miss the 1970 season because of an injury. What was it?

7 The Green Bay Packers tried to use former Cowboys punter Ron Widby at another position, but an injury ended his career. At which position were the Packers using Widby?

8 He played with a broken collarbone in a playoff game against San Francisco.

9 An injury kept him at home before a plane crash wiped out his Cal-Poly football team.

10 Which Los Angeles Rams linebacker put Roger Staubach out of action during the 1972 season?

11 This player could have used his own hospital during the 1974 season. He had ankle surgery in June and a broken rib in August. He was also slowed by a cracked rib and an infected elbow. Who was he?

12 Where was Benny Barnes on opening day in 1980?

13 What was Roger Staubach's relationship with the Philadelphia Eagles' Mel Tom in 1971?

14 Name the three Cowboy running backs who made headlines with their toes.

15 Whose rib-cracking tackle of Eagles quarterback Ron Jaworski earned a penalty and a fine?

16 What happened to Toni Fritsch after he had replaced Mike Clark as the Cowboys' regular kicker in 1971?

17 Why did teammates yell "clang" when Charlie Waters made a tackle?

18 Who missed playing time in 1979 because of a mirror?

19 He missed playing time in his final season because of nagging back problems. The injury helped convince him to retire after the Silver Season. Who was he?

20 He suffered the worst frostbite on the team but managed to score one of the Cowboys' touchdowns in the "Ice Bowl."

21 A No. 1 draft pick, this Cowboy was considered to be progressing as a fine defensive player and was expected to play a key role on the team. But a neck injury during his rookie year forced him to retire.

22 Another No. 1 draft pick, this center was being groomed to take over for John Fitzgerald. He was even being counted on as a possible All-Pro performer before knee problems ended his career.

23 This three-time All-Pro receiver saw his career cut short by an injury — not on the field, but in a car accident during the off-season. Who was he?

24 After being cut in 1983, he regained a place on the roster when James Jones went on injured reserve.

25 He was cut in training camp in 1981 but returned to the roster when Mike Hegman broke his arm.

26 He was also cut in 1981 but came back when Don Smerek suffered a knee injury in the second regular-season game.

27 After coming to Dallas in a trade from Pittsburgh in 1964, this outstanding receiver missed most of the year with an injury.

28 He was leading the team in receiving and touchdowns in 1973 when he suffered a broken ankle in the seventh game.

29 How did Drew Pearson have his consecutive game streak broken at 100 in 1979?

30 Why did Steve Wilson return to the Cowboys after being cut in training camp in 1979?

31 How did Charlie Waters have his consecutive game streak broken in 1979?

Drew Pearson

111

DALLAS COWBOYS TRIVIA **62** **CHALLENGE CONTEST!**

This kicker missed the entire 1974 season with a knee injury.

A. Duane Carroll. **B.** Rafael Septien. **C.** Toni Fritsch. **D.** Efren Herrera.

(IS THERE A DOCTOR IN THE HOUSE? — ANSWERS)

Just stay away from mirrors, Tony.

A

1 A broken bone in his foot.

2 Dan Reeves, who had a finger poked in his eye.

3 Perkins broke a toe and was out for the season.

4 Randy Hughes.

5 Hill went back to the backfield because Dan Reeves was coming off knee surgery (and Don Perkins had retired).

6 Gaechter suffered a torn Achilles' tendon.

7 Wide receiver.

8 Walt Garrison.

9 Fred Whittingham.

10 Marlin McKeever.

11 Roger Staubach.

12 In a Washington hospital recuperating from an appendectomy.

13 Tom knocked Staubach unconscious in his first start of the year.

14 Don Perkins injured his toe prior to joining the team, while getting ready to play for the College All-Stars; Calvin Hill was plagued throughout his career with bouts of "turf toe"; and Tony Dorsett suffered a broken toe in 1979.

15 Dennis Thurman.

16 Fritsch pulled a hamstring and lost the job back to Clark.

17 Waters had a steel rod in his shoulder from a previous injury.

18 Tony Dorsett. A mirror given to him by a fan fell on his toe, putting him out of action.

19 Bob Breunig.

20 George Andrie.

21 Billy Cannon Jr.

22 Robert Shaw.

23 Drew Pearson. By the way, he considered a comeback attempt prior to the 1985 season, but was advised by doctors not to play again for fear of risking further damage.

24 Cleo Simmons.

25 Angelo King.

26 Bruce Thornton.

27 Buddy Dial.

28 Otto Stowe.

29 He hurt himself when he landed wrong after spiking the ball following a touchdown against the New York Giants and was sidelined the next week in Philadelphia.

30 He replaced Butch Johnson, who was out with a broken finger.

31 He was injured during a pre-season game and missed the entire year.

Randy Hughes — what might have been.

FRIEND OR FOE

Most of the original members of the Dallas Cowboys came to the team through the expansion draft and over the years, many other opponents joined the team through trades or free agency. Of course, some Cowboys have gone on to other teams . . . as players or coaches.

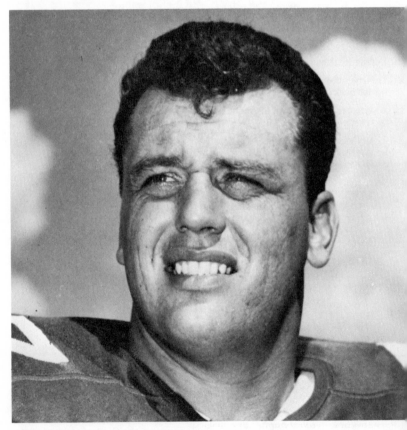

Jim Colvin, the former Baltimore Colt.

1 Which team was the victim of six of Drew Pearson's 100-yard receiving games?

2 The trade of linebacker Tom Stincic in 1973 provided Dallas with a third-round draft pick. Who did they select with that pick?

3 When Dallas traded Jerry Rhome, who did it select with the draft choice it got in that deal?

4 What was the first team the Cowboys beat in 1962?

5 Tex Schramm introduced a Hall of Fame inductee in 1985 at Canton, Ohio, who wasn't a Cowboy or former Cowboy. Who was he?

6 Where did former rival George Allen rate Danny White among NFL quarterbacks in his article for "TV Guide" in 1985?

7 How many passes did former foe Harold Carmichael catch for the Cowboys?

8 Which team was able to break Dallas' hold on first place in the selling of NFL Properties merchandise between 1977 and '84?

9 Which player came to Dallas from Baltimore in exchange for defensive lineman Guy Reese?

10 In his last two games against Dallas in 1963, before joining the Cowboys in 1964, he had four touchdown catches. Who was he?

11 He succeeded retired Art Donovan on the line at Baltimore in 1962, before joining the Cowboys in a 1964 trade.

12 This former Marine from Colorado came to Dallas in the middle of the 1964 season from the Canadian Football League.

13 After catching more than 200 passes in his first five years in the NFL, he was plagued by injuries in Dallas and caught just 42 during his three-year stay.

14 Who was Pete Gent's backup in the mid-1960s?

15 Where did the Cowboys get Danny Villanueva?

16 This North Carolina A&T-ex was a late acquisition from the San Francisco 49ers — and one of the most experienced players on the Dallas roster — in 1965.

17 After six straight regular-season losses to this team, the Cowboys finally won for the first time in 1963.

18 This team also won the first six meetings against Dallas, but two of the games were playoffs. Which team held this edge?

19 Don Meredith set a record for most consecutive passes without an interception (166) in 1965 and '66. Did the Cowboys lose any games during the streak?

20 He scored 24 points against the Cowboys in one game in 1961. Who was he?

21 The individual record for most points against Dallas in a game hasn't been broken, but it was tied by a well-known Los Angeles receiver in 1973. Who was he?

22 Who had the best rushing game against the Cowboys, Earl Campbell, Jim Brown, or Wilbert Montgomery?

23 This one-time Cowboy once scored 100 points in a single season for the Chicago Bears.

24 This New York Giants linebacker helped out at Cowboys' camp during his college days at Cal Lutheran in the 1970s.

25 This member of the Cowboys' organization played against Tom Landry in college.

26 They each scored two touchdowns against the Cowboys in Dallas' first playoff game.

27 The Cowboys-Redskins rivalry

DALLAS COWBOYS TRIVIA **63** CHALLENGE CONTEST!

Who was the only player picked ahead of Randy White in the 1975 draft?
A. Steve Bartkowski. **B.** Earl Campbell. **C.** Wilbert Montgomery.
D. Danny White.

began in the 1960s, but these two players of the '70s were considered the main combatants.

28 He punted against Dallas in the 1981 NFC Championship game before joining the Cowboys in 1983.

29 He turned down a professional baseball offer to play for Cleveland in 1958 and joined the Cowboys in 1983.

30 In a 1962 game, which team scored on two 100-yard plays in the same quarter?

31 What was Chuck Howley's first professional team?

32 Who scored the last touchdown in Super Bowl V?

33 Bart Starr scored the winning touchdown in the "Ice Bowl," but had called another play in the huddle. What was it?

34 What was the score in Bart Starr's first victory as a coach?

35 What team besides Dallas drafted Bob Hayes?

36 What did Forrest Gregg say was the most important thing he took from his year with the Cowboys?

37 This scout was a member of the Cleveland Browns' all-time team as a guard.

38 What happened to Herb Adderley three days after he arrived in Dallas from Green Bay?

39 This one-time Cowboy once held the Philadelphia Eagles' record for

longest field goal (with a pair o 50-yarders).

40 This receiver was the most ex perienced player on the Cowboys first-year roster.

41 He was the San Francisco 49ers' No 1 draft choice in 1955 and joined th Cowboys in 1961.

42 What was the only team Dallas bea twice in 1961?

43 He was a member of the all-tim Cleveland Browns team and playec two years for the Cowboys.

44 Who came to Dallas in the trade fo Danny Villanueva?

45 What year did Ernie Stautner joir the Cowboys?

46 Who was the opponent and wha was the year when Billy Howto passed Don Hutson on the all-tim receiving yards list?

47 Who did Dallas get in exchange fo Mike Connelly?

48 He went to the Eagles in exchang for Jack Concannon before comin to Dallas two years later.

49 This tight end scored touchdown against the Cowboys for two othe teams before Dallas acquired him i a trade in 1969.

50 Who did Dallas send to Green Ba in exchange for Herb Adderley?

51 Who did Dallas trade to San Dieg to obtain Lance Alworth?

52 How did Dallas acquire Gloste Richardson?

Craig Morton, left, and Golden Richards.

53 Who did Dallas receive from Los Angeles in the Lance Rentzel trade?

54 Which two former Green Bay Packers played in Super Bowl VI for the Cowboys?

55 What happened to Tony Liscio after he was traded to San Diego?

56 This Cowboy scored on a 53-yard pass from Joe Namath in his second professional game.

57 To which team did the Cowboys trade Craig Morton?

58 How did John Niland end his career with Dallas?

59 Did Dallas trade Clint Longley to Cincinnati or San Diego?

60 Where did the Cowboys send Jay Saldi?

61 Which team did Jean Fugett play for after leaving Dallas?

62 To which team did the Cowboys trade Golden Richards?

63 How did Dallas obtain John Dutton?

64 For which team did Preston Pearson play immediately before coming to Dallas?

65 Where did he play before that?

66 What was the last year for George Allen to face the Cowboys as the Redskins' coach?

67 This former Dallas quarterback had his first 3,000-yard passing season in 1981 with another team. Name him and the team.

68 He was traded at mid-season in 1974 and started seven games for another team that same year.

69 Who had a longer string of consecutive pass attempts without an interception, Craig Morton or Don Meredith?

70 Why was third-round pick Bill Roe the Cowboys' first draft choice in 1980?

71 This former free-agent specialty-teams player was sent from Dallas to Buffalo and then on to Denver. Who was he?

DALLAS COWBOYS TRIVIA (64) CHALLENGE CONTEST!

Which two former Dallas draft picks were quarterbacks with the Denver Broncos in 1981?

A. Craig Morton and Craig Penrose.   **B.** Craig Penrose and Steve DeBerg.
C. Craig Morton and Steve DeBerg.   **D.** Clint Longley and Steve DeBerg.

72 By how much time did the Cowboys beat the trading deadline when they obtained John Dutton?

73 These two former Western Athletic Conference kickers competed for the punting job in 1976 training camp.

74 He returned to Dallas in 1975 when the World Football League folded — but failed to make a successful comeback.

75 Who did Dallas get from San Diego in the trade for Duane Thomas?

76 How did Dallas acquire Otto Stowe?

77 He caught more passes in seven games for the Cowboys (23) than he did in two previous seasons in Miami.

78 Dallas acquired him from Cincinnati just a few weeks after the Bengals selected him in the 1974 supplemental draft.

79 He was the only Cowboy named as the Field Scovell Award winner by the Dallas All-Sports Association who wasn't a career Cowboy.

80 Who was the first player to rush for more than 100 yards in a game against Dallas?

81 He was a starting defensive end for four years at Green Bay before joining Dallas in 1960 — and was the only Cowboy from Indiana.

82 Which two teams did Billy Howton play for before coming to the Cowboys?

83 He scored a 70-yard touchdown against the Cowboys in their first regular-season game — and later played for Dallas.

84 He kicked four field goals against Dallas in the first meeting with the Redskins to lead Washington to a 26-14 victory.

85 He was the No. 2 draft pick in 197 but never played for Dallas.

86 The Cowboys won their first 1 games in Texas Stadium. Which team beat them in the 11th game?

DALLAS COWBOYS TRIVIA (65) CHALLENGE CONTEST!

Who were the 100-yard rushers the first time Dallas had two in one game?

A. Robert Newhouse and Duane Thomas.
B. Walt Garrison and Calvin Hill.
C. Calvin Hill and Duane Thomas.
D. Walt Garrison and Robert Newhouse.

87 Who was the opponent in 1978 when Tony Dorsett and Robert Newhouse both rushed for more than 100 yards?

88 When was the first time two Cowboys rushed for more than 100 yards in a single game?

89 He was released by the Rams in 1978, joined the Cowboys, and led the team in scoring.

90 Only two players finished ahead of Tony Dorsett in NFL rushing in 1978. Who were they?

91 Who was the opponent in 1979 when Tony Dorsett ran for three touchdowns?

92 Only two running backs gained more yards in the first eight years of their careers than Tony Dorsett did in his first eight with Dallas. Name them.

at Toomay, before the book.

*Before he joined the Cowboys, Lance Alworth was one of
the AFC's all-time greats.*

93 Who was the first quarterback to
complete four touchdown passes
against Dallas?

94 This former Baylor lineman came to
Dallas in trade for Monte Clark.

95 Which team gained more than 5[
yards total offense against Dallas
the Cowboys' first season?

96 In their first year, the Cowbo
played one game in which th

didn't fumble. Who was the opponent?

97 What was Dallas' best defensive game in 1960?

98 Did Hall of Famer Jim Brown have a 100-yard rushing game in his first meeting with the Cowboys?

99 Which Cleveland Brown player scored on a 46-yard pass reception, a 30-yard run, and a 90-yard kickoff runback in the Browns' first game against Dallas?

100 This quarterback attempted the most passes against Dallas in the Cowboys' first year. He later became known in another profession. Who was he?

101 Which team scored touchdowns on interception and kickoff returns against Dallas in the Cowboys' first year?

102 Who were the league's 1,000-yard rushers in the Cowboys' first season?

103 In which conference did the Cowboys compete in their second season?

104 Which team did Dallas finish ahead of that second season?

105 Dallas had the misfortune to have two fumbles returned for touchdowns in one game in 1961. Who was the opponent?

106 To which team did Dallas trade Dick Bielski in 1962?

107 Who was the first opponent to pass for five touchdowns against Dallas?

108 Who was the first to pass for six?

109 From which team did Dallas acquire Sam Baker in 1962?

110 This player was the first to return an interception against Don Meredith for a touchdown.

111 This 6-5 tight end came to Dallas from Green Bay and caught 39 passes (including six for touch-

COWBOYS

JAY SALDI

A friend — and later a foe.

downs) in 1962.

112 He was acquired when Dallas sent Jim Boeke to New Orleans.

113 He led the Los Angeles Rams in kickoff returns in 1954.

114 This running back went to Denver the same year the Broncos got another former Cowboy, Craig Morton.

115 Who was the former Detroit draft pick who joined the Cowboys in 1974 when Dallas needed place-kicking help?

116 Which team held Dallas to just eight first downs in 1960?

117 Three teams scored more than 40 points against Dallas in the first season. Which team scored the most points?

118 In NFL composite standings, which teams did Dallas finish ahead of in 1961?

119 In 1961, this opponent returned two interceptions for touchdowns in St. Louis' 31-17 victory.

120 Dallas intercepted five of his passes in 1968.

121 This St. Louis duo combined for a 78-yard pass play against Dallas in 1961.

122 A native of Midland, Texas, he signed with Dallas after being cut by Miami.

123 How did the Cowboys obtain Eddie LeBaron?

124 How did they get Don Meredith?

125 In February 1963, the Cowboys lost their biggest rivals. What happened?

126 Which team was the victim of seven of Roger Staubach's fourth-quarter comebacks, St. Louis or Washington?

130 Who was the first career Cowboy to score against the Cowboys?

131 Who did Thomas Henderson say couldn't spell cat?

132 Which former Cowboy went to the Canadian Football League and later played for and helped coach the Shreveport team in the American Football Association?

133 Which AFL team drafted Roger Staubach?

134 Who was Jairo Penaranda?

135 Who was the first player the Cowboys went to court for in a battle against the American Football League?

136 Before joining the Cowboys, this player was an original member of the Los Angeles Rams' Fearsome Foursome.

DALLAS COWBOYS TRIVIA **66** **CHALLENGE CONTEST!**

This former Cowboy was later named AFC Player of the Year.

A. Calvin Hill.   **B.** Craig Morton.   **C.** Todd Christensen.   **D.** Rod Hill.

127 Which NFC running back beat Calvin Hill by two yards for the 1973 rushing crown?

137 He was an All-Pro with the Ottawa Roughriders before joining the Cowboys.

DALLAS COWBOYS TRIVIA **67** **CHALLENGE CONTEST!**

Which was the last team to beat Dallas in the Cowboys' first World Championship season?

A. Miami.   **B.** San Francisco.   **C.** Minnesota.   **D.** Chicago.

128 Who was the defender who was knocked down trying to cover the famous Roger Staubach Hail Mary pass?

129 Who was the owner of the cross-town rivals from the AFL?

138 He backed up Paul Warfield at Miami before joining the Cowboys.

139 Dallas traded them for a draft pick to get Robert Newhouse.

140 Which teams have the Cowboy

Jack Patera knew the value of a good pose.

Herb Adderley

Calvin Hill

played three times in one season?

141 This future foe was also on the opposing team when Roger Staubach played in the Ohio High School All-Star Game after his senior year.

142 This former SMU player was picked by the Cowboys from the Green Bay Packers in the expansion pool.

143 From which team did the Cowboys obtain Frank Clarke?

144 Before their game in 1967, which charges did the Cowboys and Rams make against each other?

145 What was the significance of the Cardinals' victory over Dallas in their ABC "Monday Night Football" game in 1970?

146 If not for a court decision, th Cowboy would have wound up wi the Houston Oilers.

147 Pro Bowl performer Pat Donov was obtained with a draft pick as t result of a trade involving whi former Cowboy?

148 Dallas traded draft picks and th wide receiver to Seattle for the pi that brought Tony Dorsett to t Cowboys.

149 Which player did Dallas trade Seattle for the pick that gave t Cowboys Doug Cosbie?

150 Which teams have never beat Dallas in regular-season play?

151 Who broke the Cowboys' string opening day victories in 1982?

DALLAS COWBOYS TRIVIA 68 CHALLENGE CONTEST!

What Cowboy played in five Super Bowls — not all for Dallas?

A. Lance Alworth. **B.** Forrest Gregg. **C.** Preston Pearson
D. Herb Adderley.

(FRIEND OR FOE — ANSWERS)

A

1 Dallas' old rival, the Washington Redskins.

2 Harvey Martin in the third round.

3 Charlie Waters, in 1970 in the third round.

4 Los Angeles, 27-17. Dallas went on to win five games.

5 Pete Rozelle, a former associate of Schramm's at Los Angeles.

6 Eighth overall.

7 None.

8 Pittsburgh in 1980. Dallas was the leader every other year.

9 Defensive lineman Jim Colvin.

10 Buddy Dial (he came from Pittsburgh).

11 Jim Colvin.

12 Bill Frank.

13 Buddy Dial.

14 Again, Buddy Dial.

15 From the Los Angeles Rams.

16 Running back J.D. Smith.

17 St. Louis.

18 Green Bay (in fact, Dallas didn't beat the Packers in the regular season until 1970).

19 No; they won all three games in 1965 and the first four in '66. When the streak ended against St. Louis, the Cowboys and Cardinals tied, 10-10.

20 Dick James of Washington; the record is still on the books.

21 Harold Jackson.

22 Brown once ran for 232; Campbell for 195. Montgomery had 194 in a playoff game for the record in that category.

23 Mac Percival.

24 Brian Kelley.

25 Scout Bob Griffin (he played quarterback at Baylor).

26 Jerry Hill and Jimmy Orr for Baltimore in the 1965 Playoff Bowl.

27 Roger Staubach and Diron Talbert.

28 Jim Miller.

29 Coach Jim Shofner.

30 Dallas (on a kickoff return and interception return against Philadelphia).

31 The Chicago Bears.

32 Baltimore's Ed Nowatzke.

33 A handoff to Chuck Mercein.

34 Green Bay 19, Dallas 17.

35 The Denver Broncos.

36 The opportunity to work in and learn a system different from the one in Green Bay.

37 John Wooten.

38 He started in a game against the New York Jets.

39 Dick Bielski.

40 Woodley Lewis (with 11 years in the NFL).

41 Dickie Maegle.

42 Minnesota (21-7 and 28-0).

43 Jim Ray Smith.

44 Tommy McDonald; he played wide receiver for one year.

45 In 1966 (he ended his playing career in 1964).

46 Washington in 1963.

47 Kicker Mike Clark.

48 Mike Ditka.

49 Mike Ditka; he scored for Chicago and Philadelphia against the Cowboys.

Jackie Smith, long before his most famous play.

50 Malcolm Walker and Clancy Williams.

51 Pettis Norman, Tony Liscio, and Ron East.

52 In a trade with Kansas City for Dennis Homan.

53 Billy Truax and Wendell Tucker.

54 Herb Adderley and Lee Roy Caffey.

55 He was later traded to Miami, retired, and then signed with the Cowboys midway through the 197 season.

56 Bob Hayes — in the 1965 Senior Bowl.

57 The New York Giants.

58 He was traded to Philadelphia in 1975.

59 He was traded to San Diego; he was obtained from Cincinnati.

60 He was traded to Chicago after the 1982 season.

61 The Redskins.

62 Chicago.

63 In a trade with Baltimore.

64 The Pittsburgh Steelers.

65 Baltimore.

66 In 1977 (Dallas won both games).

67 Craig Morton with Denver.

68 Craig Morton (he was traded to New York's Giants).

69 Meredith had 166 in a row in 1965 and '66; Morton had 144 for Denver in 1978.

70 Dallas gave Baltimore its first- and second-round draft picks for John Dutton in 1979.

71 Wade Manning.

72 By 20 minutes.

73 Mitch Hoopes and Danny White.

74 Duane Thomas.

75 Receivers Billy Parks and Mike Montgomery.

76 In a trade with Miami for Ron Sellers.

77 Otto Stowe.

78 Clint Longley.

79 Forrest Gregg.

80 John David Crow (143 yards).

81 Nate Borden.

82 The Cleveland Browns and Green Bay Packers.

83 Buddy Dial.

84 Bob Khayat kicked four field goals for the Redskins from 15, 29, 38, and 10 yards.

85 Todd Christensen.

86 San Francisco, 31-10, in 1972.

87 Green Bay (Dorsett had 149 and Newhouse 101).

88 In 1972 in a game against Washington.

89 Rafael Septien.

90 Earl Campbell and Walter Payton.

91 Minnesota (Dorsett had 145 rushing yards).

92 Jim Brown and Walter Payton.

93 Bobby Layne, in Dallas' first regular-season game.

94 Jim Ray Smith.

95 The Los Angeles Rams (506 yards).

96 Washington.

97 The Cowboys held St. Louis to just 12 points, but still lost, 12-10.

98 No, he gained just 25 yards on seven carries.

99 Bobby Mitchell.

100 John Brodie of San Francisco, later a television announcer, he attempted 29 passes.

101 Cleveland (Bobby Mitchell had the kick return and Larry Stephens made the interception runback).

102 Jim Brown, Jim Taylor, and John David Crow.

103 Eastern.

104 Washington (the Redskins were 1-12-1; Dallas was 4-9-1).

105 Cleveland (Bernie Parrish and Vince Costello scored).

106 Dallas traded him to Baltimore; it was a three-way deal in which the Cowboys received Jerry Norton from St. Louis.

107 Sonny Jurgensen, Philadelphia, 1961.

Bob Hayes, on the way to another touchdown.

108 Y.A. Tittle of New York in 1962.

109 Cleveland.

110 Johnny Sample of Pittsburgh (but the Cowboys won the game, their first, in 1961).

111 Lee Folkins.

112 Jackie Burkett.

113 Woodley Lewis.

114 Jim Jensen.

115 Efren Herrera.

116 Cleveland.

117 Cleveland (48).

118 Washington, Los Angeles, and Minnesota.

119 Bill Stacy.

120 King Hill.

121 Sam Etcheverry and Tex Anderson.

122 Brad Wright.

123 From Washington in exchange for first- and sixth-round draft choices in 1961.

124 From Chicago in exchange for a 1962 third-round draft pick.

125 The Dallas Texans moved to Kansas City.

126 St. Louis; Washington was only beaten twice.

127 John Brockington of Green Bay.

128 Nate Wright.

129 Lamar Hunt.

130 Robert Newhouse scored against Dallas in the College All-Star game.

131 Terry Bradshaw.

132 Clint Longley.

133 Kansas City.

134 The Rams' rookie running back whe Randy Hughes was trying to tackl when he dislocated his righ shoulder for the final time.

135 Jimmy Harris.

136 Larry Stephens.

Mike Ditka played numerous roles for and against Dallas.

137 Margene Adkins.

138 Otto Stowe.

139 Halvor Hagen and Honor Jackson.

140 Washington in 1972 and Philadelphia in 1980.

141 Paul Warfield.

142 Don McIlhenny.

143 Cleveland.

144 They accused each other of spying.

145 The 38-0 victory by St. Louis was the first time Dallas was shut out in a regular-season game; it was also the last time the Cowboys lost that season until the Super Bowl.

146 Ralph Neely.

147 Mike Montgomery.

148 Duke Fergerson.

149 Bill Gregory.

150 Seattle, New England, and the New York Jets.

151 Pittsburgh's Steelers.

AUTHOR, AUTHOR

Even before the "America's Team" label was hung on the Dallas Cowboys, the team was the subject of numerous books and magazine features. More than 20 years after the first Cowboys book was published, they're still rolling off the presses — and these days, several former players are among the authors.

Q

1 What was the name of Tim Panaccio's book detailing the Dallas Cowboys-Washington Redskins rivalry?

2 Who wrote the introduction to the book, "A Decade of Dreams"?

3 Which game did former Washington Redskins coach George Allen single out as his greatest effort in the book, "Pro Football at its Best"?

4 Who was pictured on the back cover of "Texas Sport: The Illustrated History?"

5 Who wrote "Milk For Babes"?

6 What was the name of PR director Doug Todd's first book?

7 In 1980, he was featured on the cover of "Grit."

8 Who wrote the histories of the cattlemen and real-life cowboys that were featured on the covers of the 1961 Dallas Cowboys home-game programs?

9 He wrote for the "Garland Daily News" during the off-season in the late 1970s.

10 He authored a sports-related column for "Dallas-Fort Worth Business Weekly."

11 These two players kept diaries that were used by newspapers during Super Bowl XII.

12 A former Dallas quarterback went into the publishing game with an annual pre-draft magazine that carried his name.

13 Who wrote "The Crunch"?

14 This former Dallas lineman put together a book of photos of his teammates and his days with the Cowboys. His name is part of the title.

15 Who wrote "When All The Laughter Died In Sorrow"?

16 Which eight Dallas Cowboys were

DALLAS COWBOYS TRIVIA **69** **CHALLENGE CONTEST!**

What game did Vince Lombardi single out as his greatest in the book, "Pro Football at its Best"?

A. His first win over Dallas (26-14) in 1960. **B.** The 1967 NFL Championship game, which the Packers won by a 21-17 score in Green Bay. **C.** The 1966 NFL Championship, which the Packers won, 34-27, in the Cotton Bowl. **D.** The 34-0 loss to Dallas in his second season at Washington.

singled out in George Allen's book, "Pro Football's 100 Greatest Players"?

7 Who wrote "Next Year's Champions"?

3 What was the name of Steve Perkins' book about the Dallas Cowboys' first Super Bowl championship season?

9 Who wrote "Landry ... The Man Inside"?

0 Bob St. John wrote an early Dallas Cowboys history, in 1972, for "Sport Magazine Press." What was it called?

1 What was the name of Carlton Stowers' history of the Dallas Cowboys' first 25 years?

2 This linebacker's wife compiled the "Cowboys' Wives' Family Fitness Guide and Nutritional Cookbook."

3 Who wrote "Dallas Cowboys: Pro or Con," an early history (published in 1970)?

4 What was the name of Bobbi Field's book about the wives of members of the Dallas Cowboys?

5 Whose book referred to first down?

6 Which member of the Cowboys' Kick Karavan wrote "The Kicking Game"?

7 Who wrote the foreword to "Dallas Cowboys: The First Twenty-Five Years"?

8 Who wrote "Celebrity Turkey Trot" and "The Franchise"?

9 This Cowboy-turned businessman returned to writing to co-author "Winning Strategies In Selling."

0 Who was author of the book, "Journey To Triumph"?

Who authored "Time Enough To Win"?

2 What was the name of Craig Morton's first book?

3 Who was the subject of Dick Conrad's book about the first player to go from a Heisman one year to the Super Bowl the next?

34 Four members of the Cowboys had roles in "The Kicking Game." Who were they?

35 He wrote a 40-page text entitled "Keying Defenses" after leaving the Cowboys and beginning a career as a professor at Syracuse.

36 This flamboyant coverboy was interviewed by "Playboy" in its December 1981 issue.

Ben Agajanian

37 He was featured in the "Sports Hero" biographies series by Marshall and Sue Burchard.

38 He wrote a book in 1969 on football fundamentals.

39 What was "Pro File"?

40 What was the name of the anti-Dallas Cowboys book written by Miller Bonner and Mark Nelson in 1984?

41 What was the name of the Dallas Cowboys Cheerleaders story?

42 What was "Una Decada de Suenos"?

54 This newspaper, published 32 times a year, featured the Dallas Cowboys and is second in weekly circulation only to "The Sporting News."

DALLAS COWBOYS TRIVIA **70** **CHALLENGE CONTEST!**

He offered up this trivia question about himself in his autobiography: "Who was the only player ever to block a Lew Alcindor shot in college?"

A. Bruce Walton. **B.** Ed (Too Tall) Jones. **C.** Preston Pearson.
D. Pete Gent.

---

43 The "Dallas Times Herald" published a special section detailing his career when he retired.

44 Who wrote the introduction to "How To Talk Country"?

45 What was the name of Preston Pearson's autobiography?

46 He was the subject of "Pro Football Magazine's" feature, "King of the Super Bowl" prior to Super Bowl XIII.

47 In Richard Kaplan's book, "Great Upsets of the NFL" (published in 1972), which Dallas game was singled out?

48 Three Dallas games are featured in John Thorn's "Pro Football's Ten Greatest Games." Name them.

49 Who helped revise and update "Bear Bryant On Winning Football"?

50 Who helped write — and was pictured on the cover of — "The NFL Way To Play Touch Football," a Sears publication?

51 Which member of the Cowboys was featured in "The Game-Makers" by Jack Clary?

52 What was the name of the Putnam Sports Shelf book about Bob Hayes?

53 Who was featured in the February 1981 issue of "Money" magazine?

55 What is the hardback publication that is the public version of the Cowboys' media guide?

56 Which "Sports Illustrated" writer picked the Cowboys to win their conference championship in 1963?

57 A forerunner of the Dallas Cowboys weekly newspaper, this publication carried the name of one of the players.

Lance Rentzel

8 He was featured in a 1973 Spire Christian Comics publication.

9 What team was featured in the 1982 Sanger-Harris/Dallas Times Herald Marvel Comics special?

0 In October 1972, "Life" magazine did a story on "Rough, Tough Pros." Who was featured on the cover, bare-chested and scowling?

1 Who was featured on the cover of the inaugural edition of "The Dallas Cowboys" magazine?

2 He made an appearance on the cover of "Boy's Life" magazine in November 1962 — and again in November 1977.

3 Who was the first Dallas Cowboys quarterback featured on a "Sports Illustrated" cover?

64 He was a "Texas Business" coverboy in 1980.

65 This former quarterback was a writer for a weekly paper in Rockwall, Texas.

66 Who was featured in the 1974 Tempo Books "Great Running Backs #2"?

67 In a "Pro" feature by Stan Lee and John Buscema comparing NFL linebackers to Marvel Comics characters, who was featured as Captain America?

68 Who was featured on the 1971 Southwest Edition of the "Complete Handbook Of Pro Football"?

69 Frank Ryan's wife, in a column for the "Cleveland Plain Dealer," called this Cowboys quarterback a loser.

70 Who is Phil Musick?

(AUTHOR, AUTHOR — ANSWERS)

1 "Cowboys An' Indians." It was billed as "the story of pro football's most combative rivalry."

2 Tex Schramm put some of his writing skills to use again.

3 The 1972 NFC Championship. It figures, since his team won that one, 26-3.

4 Don Meredith. Tom Landry, Lance Alworth, Harvey Martin, Bob Lilly, Jerry Rhome, and Tex Schramm were pictured inside.

5 Anne Murchison — wife of former owner Clint Murchison.

6 "How To Talk Country."

7 Roger Staubach.

8 The late "Dallas Morning News" writer Frank X. Tolbert.

9 Former Wyoming cornerback Aaron Kyle.

10 Preston Pearson.

11 Aaron Kyle kept one for the "Dallas Times Herald" and Pat Donovan wrote his for the "New York Times."

12 Don Heinrich — the magazine was called "Don Heinrich's Scout Report."

13 Former defensive lineman Pat Toomay. The book was published in 1975, after Toomay had left Dallas.

14 Bob Lilly. The book was "Bob Lilly: Reflections."

15 Lance Rentzel.

16 Allen considered Cliff Harris, Mike Ditka, Roger Staubach, Lance Alworth, Herb Adderley, Forrest Gregg, Bob Lilly, and Randy White among the "100 greatest" of all time.

17 Steve Perkins, then with the "Dallas Times Herald."

18 "Winning The Big One."

19 "Dallas Morning News" sportswriter Bob St. John.

20 "We Love You Cowboys."

21 "Dallas Cowboys: The First Twenty-Five Years."

22 Bob Breunig's wife, Mary, was the creator and editor of the book. Proceeds go to Happy Hill Farm children's home in Glen Rose.

23 Sam Blair of the "Dallas Morning News."

24 "The Dallas Cowboys Super Wives."

25 Roger Staubach's "Staubach: First Down, Lifetime To Go."

A Marvel-ous story.

26 Former NFL kicker Ben Agajani (with Paul T. Owens).

27 James Michener. The famous auth said his association with the tea began with his friendship with D Meredith.

28 Pete Gent. Of course, his first eff — "North Dallas Forty" — was bett known than the other two.

29 Roger Staubach.

30 All-time Dallas Cowboys' expe Carlton Stowers.

31 Former great Roger Staubach.

32 "The Courage To Believe" (Rob Burger was co-author).

33 Tony Dorsett in "Sports Stars To Dorsett: From Heisman To Sup Bowl In One Year."

34 Tom Landry wrote the forewo Efren Herrera, Danny White, a

Pete Gent

Rafael Septien were featured in the book.

Jim Ridlon.

Thomas Henderson.

Roger Staubach.

Bob Lilly — the book was "Bob Lilly's All-Pro Football Fundamentals."

The Dallas Cowboys' PR department's newsletter for season ticket holders.

"The Semi-Official Dallas Cowboys Haters' Handbook."

"A Decade Of Dreams."

The Spanish version of the Dallas Cowboys Cheerleaders book.

Roger Staubach, of course.

A virtual expert — Walt Garrison.

"Hearing The Noise: My Life In The NFL."

Preston Pearson.

Kaplan named the Dallas-Green Bay 1967 championship, the "Ice Bowl," as one of the top 10 upsets of all time.

The January 1, 1967, Green Bay vs. Dallas game, the December 31, 1967, Green Bay vs. Dallas game, and the December 16, 1979, Washington vs. Dallas game.

Gene Stallings, a one-time Bryant assistant.

Roger Staubach.

Tom Landry.

"The Speed King: Bob Hayes Of The Dallas Cowboys."

Drew Pearson.

"Dallas Cowboys Weekly."

"The Official Dallas Cowboys Bluebook."

Tex Maule. In the same issue, the Cowboys were featured on the cover for the first time.

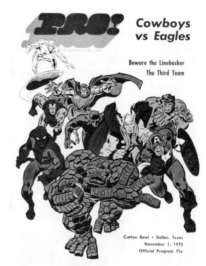

Beware the linebacker.

57 "Bob Lilly's Pro Report."

58 Tom Landry — the comic was entitled "Tom Landry and the Dallas Cowboys."

59 The Dallas Cowboys Cheerleaders. Spider-Man and the Incredible Hulk helped rescue the missing Cheerleaders.

60 Bob Lilly.

61 Don Meredith.

62 Roger Staubach.

63 Roger Staubach — in 1963 as a Midshipman.

64 Clint Murchison.

65 Clint Longley.

66 Calvin Hill, Ron Johnson, Mercury Morris, and Floyd Little.

67 Chuck Howley.

68 Duane Thomas.

69 Don Meredith.

70 Author of the "Tony Dorsett Story."

THROW IT TO ME!

What's more impressive, nine catches for 246 yards or six for 195? What ab
six catches for 187 yards — and four touchdowns?

All those numbers belong to Bob Hayes, one of the Cowboys' lead
receivers of all time. His best game (the 246 yards) came against Washing
in 1966. The four-touchdown day was against Houston four years later.

Here's a list of the top 10 receiving days in Dallas Cowboys history:

246 yards — Bob Hayes at Washington, Nov. 13, 1966 (9 catches).
241 yards — Frank Clarke vs. Washington, Sept. 16, 1962 (10).
223 yards — Lance Rentzel vs. Washington, Nov. 19, 1967 (13).
213 yards — Tony Hill vs. Philadelphia, Nov. 12, 1979 (7).
195 yards — Bob Hayes vs. N.Y. Giants, Sept. 18, 1966 (6).
190 yards — Frank Clarke at San Francisco, Nov. 10, 1963 (8).
188 yards — Drew Pearson at Detroit, Oct. 6, 1975 (6).
187 yards — Bob Hayes vs. Houston, Dec. 20, 1970 (6).
181 yards — Tony Hill at Detroit, Sept. 15, 1985 (11).
177 yards — Bob Hayes vs. Philadelphia, Oct. 10, 1965 (8).

Tony Hill — another catch for 'The Thrill.'

rew Pearson — to the victor belongs the spike.

AGAINST ALL ODDS

The Dallas Cowboys have appeared in a record five Super Bowls and, obvio[us]ly, have made numerous playoff-game appearances. Since 1966, Dallas has [had] plenty of chances to fight the odds — making three dozen post-season [ap]pearances. As many coaches will admit, the playoff games leading up to [the] Super Bowl are often more difficult than the Super Bowl itself.

Q

1 What was the score in Dallas' first playoff contest?

2 On what field was the "Ice Bowl" played?

3 In the Cowboys' first NFL Championship game, which player drew a five-yard penalty after Dallas had a first-and-goal at Green Bay's 1-yard line?

4 Who threw the 50-yard touchdo[wn] pass that put the Cowboys ahead [in] the fourth quarter of the "Ice Bo[wl]" game?

5 Who won the "Ice Bowl" and w[hat] was the score?

6 Who made the lead block for t[he] Packers' game-winning touchdown[?]

December 31, 1967 — a day not fit for man nor beast.

the final seconds of the "Ice Bowl" — and who scored the TD?

7 Over which Cowboy was the winning touchdown scored?

8 Who scored a touchdown on an interception return in the Cowboys' first NFC Championship game shutout?

9 What was featured on Cowboys playoff game programs in the late 1970s?

10 What year did Dallas go to the Super Bowl as a wild-card team?

11 What tie-breaker gave the division title to the Cowboys over the Redskins after the two teams finished tied for first in 1973?

12 Because of the tie-breaker situation in 1973, the Cowboys went into the final game of the year against the Redskins needing to win by a wider margin than Washington had won by (14-7) in their first meeting. What was the score in the final game?

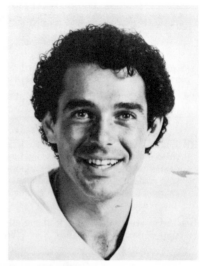

Rafael Septien

DALLAS COWBOYS TRIVIA **71** CHALLENGE CONTEST!

How many playoff games did Dallas participate in during the team's first 26 years?

A. 13.   **B.** 24.   **C.** 36.   **D.** 39.

---

13 What was the lowest score in a Dallas playoff game?

14 Who was the opponent and what was the score in the only NFC Championship game shutout of the 1970s?

15 What was the temperature at game time in the "Ice Bowl"?

16 Which Cowboy scored a touchdown on a 63-yard punt return in the 1973 NFC Championship game?

17 Which teams did Dallas beat in NFC Championship games to reach its first five Super Bowls?

18 The Cowboys were 0-2 against two teams in NFC playoff games. Name the teams.

19 What were the results of Dallas' second appearance in the Playoff Bowl?

20 What years did Dallas win two post-season games but fail to reach the Super Bowl?

21 What reason did Vince Lombardi give for the Packers going for the winning touchdown instead of attempting a tying field goal in the "Ice Bowl?"

DALLAS COWBOYS TRIVIA **72** CHALLENGE CONTEST!

Who holds the Cowboys record for most consecutive passes thrown in playoff games without an interception?
A. Don Meredith. **B.** Danny White. **C.** Roger Staubach. **D.** Craig Morton.

22 When John Brodie completed a third-quarter touchdown pass against Dallas in the 1970 NFC Championship game, he broke a Dallas defensive string for quarters without allowing a TD. What was the record?

23 The Green Bay Packers lead the all-time series against Dallas, 8-4. Who leads the playoff series between the teams?

24 In the Cowboys' playoff games, how many times has Tony Dorsett rushed for 100 or more yards?

25 In his first 12 playoff games, how many yards did Dorsett gain?

Duane Thomas breaks through the Lions' defense.

Jim Boeke

26 This Cowboy is the No. 3 all-time playoff scorer.

27 Which Cowboy defensive player scored a touchdown in the "Ice Bowl?"

28 Bill Simpson and Charlie Waters share which playoff record?

29 Which two Cowboys have scored on 80-yard receptions in playoff games?

30 Which Cowboy quarterback had the most long passes (50 yards or more) in the playoffs?

31 Which non-quarterback had a 49-yard completion to Tony Hill in the 1982-83 playoffs?

32 Who is the only Cowboy to have back-to-back 100-yard rushing games in the playoffs?

33 How many times have the Cowboys shut out an opponent in the playoffs?

34 He caught passes in every playoff game in which he participated.

35 In how many playoff games did Drew Pearson participate?

36 When did Danny White have his first 300-yard game?

37 How many passes did Everson Walls intercept in his first NFC Championship game?

38 He returned a blocked field goal 60 yards for a touchdown in the final regular-season game of 1965 to help Dallas into post-season play for the first time.

39 He recovered a fumble and intercepted two passes in the 1978 NFC Championship game.

40 He had a 68-yard touchdown on a pass interception in the same game.

41 Which of those two players had earlier set the Cowboy record for most interceptions in a single playoff game?

42 Which one of the two defensive standouts in that 1978 game also starred two years earlier (in a loss to Los Angeles) with an interception and two blocked punts?

43 Which two teams did Dallas beat in the playoffs prior to Super Bowl XII?

44 What did Vince Lombardi do before the "Ice Bowl" to combat a frozen field?

45 Who was the first Cowboy to pass for 300 yards in a playoff game?

46 Who was the first receiver to total more than 100 yards in a single playoff game?

47 Who was the first 100-yard rusher in a playoff game for Dallas?

48 Name the only Cowboy to rank among the team's top five in three individual statistical categories in playoff games.

49 One other Cowboy ranks among the top 10 in three categories. Name him.

50 Who had the best average per carry in playoff games?

51 Dallas was eliminated from the playoffs in 1979 on a tipped pass. Who was the victim?

52 Who was the starting quarterback in the 1968 Eastern Conference Championship game?

53 Who engineered the only offensive drive (for a touchdown) in that game?

54 Who holds the NFL record for most playoff games played?

55 His teammate is second on the a— time list. Name him.

56 How many playoff games did Lar— Cole participate in?

(AGAINST ALL ODDS — ANSWERS)

A

1 The Baltimore Colts beat Dallas, 35-3.

2 Lambeau Field in Green Bay, Wisconsin.

3 Tackle Jim Boeke.

4 Dan Reeves completed the pass to Lance Rentzel.

5 Green Bay, 21-17.

6 Jerry Kramer made the block — and Bart Starr scored.

7 Jethro Pugh.

8 Thomas Henderson.

9 Souvenir stickers.

10 In 1975.

11 Point differential.

12 Dallas won, 27-7.

13 Dallas beat Detroit, 5-0, in 1970 playoff action.

14 Dallas beat Los Angeles, 28-0.

15 13-below zero.

16 Golden Richards.

17 Dallas beat San Francisco twice, the Los Angeles Rams twice and Minnesota once.

18 Green Bay and Washington.

19 Dallas beat Minnesota, 17-13.

20 In 1980 and '82.

21 Lombardi said he didn't want the fans to suffer through a sudden-death

overtime period in that weather a— that the Packers did not deserve to — champions if they couldn't score t— touchdown.

22 The Cowboys had held their o— ponents without a touchdown in — straight quarters.

23 Green Bay, 2-1.

24 Three times — against Los Angeles 1978 and '80 and against Tampa B— in '83.

25 Exactly 1,000 yards.

26 Rafael Septien.

27 George Andrie on a fumble recovery.

28 Most playoff interceptions (nine).

29 Bob Hayes (on an 86-yarder from Do— Meredith in 1967) and Drew Pears— (on an 83-yarder from Roge— Staubach in 1973).

30 Surprisingly, Don Meredith had thr— and Roger Staubach two.

31 Drew Pearson.

32 Duane Thomas in 1970-71, on the wa— to Super Bowl V, against Detroit ar— San Francisco.

33 Three times: Detroit, 5-0, in 1970; L— Angeles, 28-0, in 1978; and Tamp— Bay, 38-0, in 1981.

34 Drew Pearson.

35 Twenty-two.

36 In the 1980 playoffs (January 4, 198—

142

against Atlanta (322 yards).

37 Two (against San Francisco in a 28-27 loss).

38 Obert Logan.

39 Charlie Waters.

40 Thomas (Hollywood) Henderson.

41 Charlie Waters with three against Chicago in 1977. Dennis Thurman later tied the mark against Green Bay in 1983.

42 Charlie Waters, again.

43 Chicago (37-7) and Minnesota (23-6).

44 He had a gridwork of wires installed under the turf to prevent the field from freezing.

45 Danny White against Atlanta in January 1981 (he's done it twice more since then).

46 Frank Clarke on Jan. 1, 1967 (four other receivers have hit 100 since then).

47 Don Perkins vs. Green Bay on Jan. 1, 1967.

48 Tony Dorsett (first in rushing, second in scoring, and tied for fourth in receiving).

49 Butch Johnson (No. 2 in punt returns, No. 4 in kickoff returns, and No. 7 in receiving).

50 Roger Staubach (a 5.7-yard average on 76 carries).

51 Mike Hegman. Billy Waddy scored on a 50-yard play after catching the tipped pass. It was the winning touchdown in the Rams' 21-19 victory.

52 Don Meredith.

53 Craig Morton (after Meredith was benched).

54 D.D. Lewis with 27 games.

55 Charlie Waters with 26.

56 Twenty-five. He's No. 3 on the all-time list.

Tony Dorsett

The aerialists.

143

SUPER TIMES

It took the Dallas Cowboys six years before they advanced to post-season play for the first time. Another five seasons passed before they reached the ultimate goal, the Super Bowl.

Dallas lost in its first Super Bowl effort, but over a nine-year period the Cowboys reached the final game five times, winning twice.

An Official Publication of the National Football League
AFC versus NFC for the NFL Championship and the Vince Lombardi Trophy
Sunday, January 21, 1979 • 4:00 P.M. • Orange Bowl Stadium, Miami, Florida $2.50

1 After he joined the Cowboys, this fan favorite and one of Dallas' top clutch players became the first to participate in Super Bowls with three different teams. Name him — and the other two teams.

2 Who were the Cowboys' first five Super Bowl opponents?

3 What was the score in Dallas' first Super Bowl appearance?

4 Who was the Most Valuable Player of Super Bowl V?

5 Who was the winning quarterback in Super Bowl V?

6 Who was the former foe who dropped an apparent touchdown pass from Roger Staubach in the end zone in Super Bowl XIII?

7 At what motel did the Cowboys stay on their first two Super Bowl visits to Miami?

The final, agonizing seconds.

DALLAS COWBOYS TRIVIA **73** CHALLENGE CONTEST!

Who were the two former Green Bay Packers who played in Super Bowl V on opposite sides after playing together in Super Bowls I and II?

A. Herb Adderley and Bill Curry.   **B.** Lance Alworth and Herb Adderley.
C. Earl Morrall and Lance Alworth.   **D.** Bill Curry and Preston Pearson.

8 What was on the cover of the program for Super Bowl X (played on Jan. 18, 1976)?

9 Who hit Steelers quarterback Terry Bradshaw on the Steelers' winning touchdown pass in Super Bowl X?

10 Who intercepted Roger Staubach's final pass of Super Bowl X?

11 Who scored the first touchdown by a defensive player in a Super Bowl?

12 Who scored to give Dallas a 6-0 lead in Super Bowl V?

13 On one of the most controversial plays in Super Bowl history, a Cowboy defender was ruled to have touched a pass between the time two offensive players touched it. (At that time, it was illegal for two offensive players to touch the ball consecutively.) Who was the defender whose tip allowed John Mackey to score Baltimore's first touchdown in Super Bowl V?

14 How much money did each Cowboy earn in Super Bowl V?

15 What was the first Super Bowl played on artificial surface?

16 When Roger Staubach was given a new automobile for winning the Most Valuable Player award in Super Bowl VI, what did he ask for?

DALLAS COWBOYS TRIVIA **74** CHALLENGE CONTEST!

Following Dallas' second Super Bowl victory, two members of the team appeared on the cover of "Sports Illustrated." Who were they?

A. Randy Hughes and Randy White. **B.** Randy White and Harvey Martin.
C. Harvey Martin and Ed (Too Tall) Jones.
D. Roger Staubach and Drew Pearson.

17 What was printed on the Cowboys' cups used in the victory party after their second Super Bowl victory?

18 What kind of rally did Tom Landry lead prior to Super Bowl V?

19 What feature do the Cowboys' Super Bowl rings have that distinguish them from all others?

20 In Super Bowl V, who actually recovered the controversial fumble by the Cowboys on the Baltimore 2-yard line — even though the Colts were awarded the ball?

21 How much time was left in Super Bowl V when Baltimore kicked the winning field goal?

A victory ride for Tom Landry after Super Bowl VI.

22 Who was the first former Olympian to play in a Super Bowl?

23 He earned Super Bowl rings with Green Bay and Dallas, but had to settle for the runner-up role in Cincinnati.

24 What was the score in the first-ever indoor Super Bowl?

25 What was the first Super Bowl seen by more than 100,000,000 television viewers?

26 What was the date of the Cowboys' first Super Bowl appearance?

27 After President Nixon called Miami coach Don Shula prior to Super Bowl VI — with a play suggestion — Tom Landry got a telegram regarding the game. Who sent Landry the message telling him he had no plans to send in any plays?

28 What incident at the Cowboys' spring team party following Super Bowl XII was out of character for Tom Landry and his players?

29 Tom Landry has a history of having surprises for the opponents, despite his conservative image. What was the gadget play used in Super Bowl XII and which players were involved?

30 Prior to Super Bowl V, which team was given the edge by virtue of its experience on artificial turf?

31 Who was the home team in Super Bowl V?

32 How many points did the Cowboys score the first two times they had the ball inside Baltimore's 10-yard line in Super Bowl V?

33 Which was the first Super Bowl that the team that scored first didn't win?

34 Who tackled Johnny Unitas to knock the Baltimore quarterback out of action in Super Bowl V?

35 Who helped Mike Hegman pick Terry Bradshaw's pocket for a touchdown in Super Bowl XIII?

36 Which Super Bowl was the first rematch in the history of the series?

37 Other than Dallas, which NFC teams won Super Bowl titles in the 1970s?

38 Who did Roger Staubach think should have been named Most Valuable Player of Super Bowl VI?

39 Who did President Carter say he bet on in Super Bowl XIII?

40 He fumbled a kickoff that led to a Pittsburgh touchdown in Super Bowl XIII.

41 Who blocked a Mitch Hoopes punt for a safety in Super Bowl X?

42 Who scored the final touchdown in Super Bowl XII?

43 Only two teams beat Dallas on its march to Super Bowl XII. Who were they?

44 Which five players were listed in passing statistics for Dallas during the Cowboys' drive to Super Bowl XII (counting regular-season and playoffs)?

45 Which two players had more than one turnover recovery against Denver in Super Bowl XII?

DALLAS COWBOYS TRIVIA **75** **CHALLENGE CONTEST!**

Who threw the final touchdown pass in Super Bow XII?

A. Roger Staubach.   **B.** Danny White.   **C.** Robert Newhouse.
D. Golden Richards.

DALLAS COWBOYS TRIVIA **76** CHALLENGE CONTEST!

He said he thought he should have been the Most Valuable Player in Super Bowl XII because of his turnover recoveries.

A. Bruce Huther.   **B.** Aaron Kyle.   **C.** Larry Cole.   **D.** Randy Hughes.

---

46 Who else had turnover recoveries in Super Bowl XII?

47 Who were the opposing head coaches in Super Bowl XII?

48 Where was the game played?

49 How many players on the 1971 Super Bowl championship team were obtained in trades that year?

50 Whose fumble of an option pass led to a Pittsburgh touchdown in Super Bowl XIII?

51 He led the team in tackles in Super Bowl XII.

52 How did Mike Hegman score his first professional touchdown?

53 What did Lee Roy Jordan single out as the turning point in Super Bowl VI?

54 Who scored the first touchdown in Super Bowl XII?

55 Who recovered Baltimore's fumble in the end zone in Super Bowl V?

56 Which uniforms did the Cowboys wear in Super Bowl V?

57 Who intercepted a pass in Super Bowl V that led to the last touchdown?

On the defense, in Super Bowl V.

DALLAS COWBOYS TRIVIA **77** **CHALLENGE CONTEST!**

This Cowboy veteran was the only player from the Cowboys' first Super Bowl team to be named All-Pro.

A. Craig Morton. **B.** Calvin Hill. **C.** Chuck Howley. **D.** Bob Lilly.

---

58 What game is generally considered the one that erased the Cowboys' "next-year's-champions" tag?

59 Which baseball team's facilities did the Cowboys use at Fort Lauderdale prior to Super Bowl XIII?

60 Who scored the first touchdown in Super Bowl VI? (Hint: He wasn't a career Cowboy.)

61 Who scored the last touchdown in that game? (The same hint applies.)

62 What did Larry Csonka do against the Cowboys in Super Bowl VI that he hadn't done all season?

63 Which team scored first in Super Bowl V?

64 Which five players participated in all of Dallas' first five Super Bowl games?

65 Which three players were on the roster for all five Cowboy Super Bowl games — but played in only four?

(SUPER TIMES — ANSWERS)

1 Preston Pearson. He also played for Baltimore and Pittsburgh.

2 Baltimore, Miami, Pittsburgh (twice), and Denver.

3 Baltimore 16, Dallas 13.

4 Chuck Howley.

5 Earl Morrall.

6 Jackie Smith.

7 The Galt Ocean Mile.

8 The Lombardi Trophy and the American flag.

9 Cliff Harris.

10 Glen Edwards.

11 Herb Adderley.

12 Mike Clark (he kicked two field goals).

13 Mel Renfro.

14 $7,500.

15 Super Bowl V.

16 A station wagon.

17 The final score.

18 A rally for the Fellowship of Christian Athletes.

19 Both rings have stars.

20 Dave Manders.

21 Five seconds.

22 Bob Hayes.

23 Forrest Gregg.

24 Dallas 27, Denver 10.

25 Super Bowl XII.

26 Jan. 17, 1971.

27 Former President Lyndon Johnson.

28 Several players threw Landry into a swimming pool.

29 An option pass — thrown by Robert Newhouse to Golden Richards. The play went for a touchdown.

Terry Bradshaw, left, and Roger Staubach.

30 Dallas. The Cowboys had played 14 of 22 games on artificial turf; Baltimore had played only three.

31 Dallas.

32 Six points; Dallas kicked a field goal each time.

33 Super Bowl V, when Dallas scored first but Baltimore won.

34 George Andrie.

35 Thomas (Hollywood) Henderson.

36 Super Bowl XIII (Dallas vs. Pittsburgh).

37 None.

38 Staubach said anybody from the offensive line deserved the Super Bowl MVP award.

39 He bet on Dallas over Pittsburgh.

40 Randy White.

41 Reggie Harrison.

42 Golden Richards.

43 St. Louis, 24-17, and Pittsburgh, 28-13. Dallas won eight games before the two-game losing streak and seven (including the playoffs) after the losses.

44 Roger Staubach, Danny White, Tony Dorsett, Robert Newhouse, and Charlie Waters. Waters didn't have a pass attempt — but was caught for a 12-yard loss on a fake field-goal play (which counted in the passing statistics).

45 Aaron Kyle (a fumble recovery and interception) and Randy Hughes (two fumble recoveries and an interception).

46 Benny Barnes and Mark Washington had interceptions; Bruce Huther

A Steeler interception spoils a Super Bowl XIII bid.

recovered a fumble.

47 Tom Landry and Red Miller.

48 In the Superdome in New Orleans.

49 Six: Lance Alworth, Lee Roy Caffey, Gloster Richardson, Billy Truax, Don Talbert, and Tony Liscio. Talbert and Liscio, of course, had been with the team before and returned through trades.

50 Drew Pearson.

51 Thomas (Hollywood) Henderson (with seven).

52 He stole the ball from Terry Bradshaw in Super Bowl XIII and ran 37 yards for a touchdown.

53 Bob Lilly's sack of Bob Griese for a 27-yard loss.

54 Tony Dorsett on a three-yard run.

55 Rookie defensive back Charlie Waters.

56 The blue jerseys, of course.

57 Rick Volk intercepted a Craig Morton pass.

58 Super Bowl VI.

59 The New York Yankees' field.

60 Lance Alworth.

61 Mike Ditka.

62 He fumbled.

63 Dallas. It marked only the second time in the history of the series that the team that scored first did not win.

64 Larry Cole, D.D. Lewis, Cliff Harris, Charlie Waters, and Rayfield Wright.

65 Roger Staubach, Jethro Pugh, and Mark Washington.

FIRST AND LAST

The first victory, the first trip to the playoffs, the first Super Bowl win ... they all played big parts in the Cowboys' history. There were also plenty of other firsts for Dallas, as well, plus some historic seconds and lasts worth mentioning.

D.D. Lewis, left, and Lee Roy Jordan.

Q

1 These three players each made their first appearance in the Pro Bowl in 1980.

2 What happened on Danny White's first NFL pass reception?

3 Who threw the pass?

4 Who won the game in Glenn Carano's first NFL start?

5 How did John Dutton score his first NFL touchdown?

6 How did Benny Barnes score his first professional touchdown?

7 What happened on the first regular-season pass completion of Glenn Carano's career?

8 How did Mike Hegman score his first regular-season pro TD?

9 Who caught Roger Staubach's last playoff pass?

10 And who caught his last touchdown pass in the regular season?

11 What did Roger Staubach do in his last professional game?

12 Who scored the first touchdown in Texas Stadium?

152

13 His first professional pass attempt in 1979 was a 30-yard touchdown to Tony Hill.

14 He became the Cowboys' first defensive back picked in the first round since Aaron Kyle in 1976.

15 After an 0-4 start, who did the Cowboys get their first win against in 1963?

16 Long before Danny White, who was the first quarterback signed from Arizona State?

17 After two ties and two losses, the Cowboys finally beat this team for the first time in 1962.

18 He scored the first home touchdown (in a pre-season game) for the Cowboys on a one-yard plunge in August 1960.

19 His 71-yard pass brought Baltimore back to beat the Cowboys in Dallas' first home game in 1960.

20 Who caught the pass?

21 Who was Dallas' first draft choice the last year Roger Staubach played?

22 What year did Tom Landry's coaching record climb above .500?

23 Who was the first — and only — Cowboy to score in Dallas' first post-season game?

24 Who was the first Cowboy to rank among the NFL's top 10 kickoff returners?

25 More than 80,000 fans saw the Cowboys in a single game in 1966. Who was the opponent?

26 Dallas began to show winning form with its first three-game streak (against St. Louis, Chicago, and the New York Giants). What year?

27 Which two teams were also victims in the Cowboys' second three-game winning streak?

28 He ranked among the NFC's top 10 interception leaders for the first time in his career in 1984 (he was tied for second).

29 What was the first year the Cowboys had a winning pre-season record?

30 Who was the first Cowboy to score eight touchdowns both rushing and receiving in one year.

31 Who scored the first NFL touchdown in the Giants' Meadowlands Stadium?

32 What was the last year the Cowboys wore stars on the shoulders of their uniforms?

33 Who was the Cowboys' first specialty-teams captain?

34 He was the only non-quarterback to throw for a touchdown on his first-ever professional pass in 1979.

35 When was the last time Bob Lilly wore his number 74?

36 Who was the last Cowboy who played in the 1960s who retired?

37 In 1982, he led the team in total tackles, the first defensive back to do so since Cliff Harris in 1976.

38 How long was Tony Dorsett's longest run in his rookie year?

39 Was Tony Dorsett the first Cowboy to rush for 200 yards in a single game?

DALLAS COWBOYS TRIVIA **78** **CHALLENGE CONTEST!**

Who was the last Olympic gold medalist drafted by the Cowboys?

A. Mel Lattany. **B.** Carl Lewis. **C.** Harold Hays. **D.** Bob Hayes.

40 Did Tony Dorsett score a touchdown in his first Cowboy game?

41 What is the significance of Oct. 24, 1971, for the Cowboys?

42 What happened to Don Meredith in his last game for the Cowboys?

43 But what about the game before that?

44 Who had the best individual rushing game for Dallas in the Cowboys' first season?

45 In the Cowboys' first regular-season victory in 1961, who scored the touchdown that put Dallas ahead for good?

46 When did Don Perkins first run for 100 yards in a game?

47 He had one of the three longest scoring plays for Dallas in 1962 — and his effort is still on the record books 24 years later.

48 What was the Cowboys' first 100-yard play?

49 Who was the first 1,000-yard receiver for Dallas?

50 When did Lee Roy Jordan first play middle linebacker for Dallas?

51 Who was the victim of Tony Dorsett's first 100-yard rushing game?

52 Who was the last player from the original 1960 players pool of 36 to retire?

53 He was one of the first real West Texas Cowboys, from Monahans, Texas.

54 He was the first player signed from the school where the Cowboys held their first training camp (Pacific, Oregon).

55 Who was the first Cowboy to score 500 points?

56. Why did Buddy Dial catch only 11 passes in his first year?

57 Did Bob Hayes score a touchdown in his first game as a Cowboy?

58 What happened the first time Bob Hayes ran with the ball?

59 Who was the first Cowboy with 200 rushing attempts in a season?

60 Who was the first Cowboy with more than 200 receiving yards in a game?

61 Which two players made their first trip to the Pro Bowl in 1967?

62 Who was the first draft pick from Mississippi Valley?

63 Which Cowboy made his first Pro Bowl appearance in 1969?

64 Who was the first linebacker to lead the team in interceptions?

65 He was the first Cowboy to score more than 100 points two years in a row.

66 Who was the first Cowboy to kick 50 field goals in his career?

67 He was the first Cowboy to rush for 100 yards in a game on just 10 carries.

68 He made his first Pro Bowl appearance in 1970.

69 Who was the first defensive lineman picked No. 1 by the Cowboys — after Bob Lilly?

70 In what year did the Cowboys first play an overtime game?

71 Who was the first cornerback ever taken by the Cowboys in the first round of the draft?

72 These four players were named to the Pro Bowl for the first time after the 1971 season.

73 Who made his first — and only — Pro Bowl appearance in the 1973 game?

74 Was Bob Hayes ever held scoreless during an entire year (with the Cowboys)?

Amos Bullocks

75 These three players participated in the Pro Bowl for the first time in 1975.

76 He made good on the first 81 PAT attempts of his Cowboys career and finished with 106 of 108.

77 Who was Dallas' leading receiver in the first pre-season?

78 When was the first time Dallas had 300 passing yards in a game?

79 Against which team did Dallas first gain 100 rushing yards?

80 Who scored Dallas' first-ever touchdown against Washington?

81 Who scored the first rushing touchdown for the Cowboys?

82 How many rushing yards did Don McIlhenny have in the first Cowboys game?

83 Who had the longest run from scrimmage for Dallas in 1962, Amos Marsh or Amos Bullocks?

84 What happened on Drew Pearson's first three professional pass attempts?

85 What happened to the last two?

86 He was the Cowboys' first starter from Temple.

87 He was one of the last players cut in 1977 — but came back when Jim Eidson underwent knee surgery.

88 He went from first place as the team's leading rusher in 1976 to just 60 yards on 12 carries in 1977.

89 These two Cowboys were in their first Pro Bowl following the 1977 season.

90 He caught three passes for more than 100 total yards in his first scrimmage as a rookie, but caught only two passes during the regular season in 1977.

91 Who was the first center ever drafted by the Cowboys?

92 What year did the Cowboys go 9-0 at Texas Stadium?

93 How long were Thomas Henderson's first three professional touchdowns?

94 Besides Tony Dorsett, who else had 100 yards rushing in a single game in 1978?

95 Danny White got one regular-season start in 1978. Who was the opponent?

96 He was the first center ever selected No. 1 by the Cowboys.

97 Which Cowboy was the first player in NCAA history to rush for 1,500 yards three times in his college career?

98 Who did Dallas beat in its first-ever overtime victory?

99 Who did Dallas lose to in its first-ever overtime loss?

100 Who was the first player to lead the team in scoring five straight years?

101 What was the only team to beat Dallas in the first 20 games in which Tony Dorsett ran for 100 or more yards?

102 Which two Cowboys were among the first five players selected in the 1974 draft?

DALLAS COWBOYS TRIVIA 79 CHALLENGE CONTEST!

Who was the first member of the Cowboys invited to play in the Pro Bowl?

A. Eddie LeBaron. **B.** Dick Bielski. **C.** Frank Clarke. **D.** Jim Doran.

103 What did Roger Staubach do in his first starting assignment for Dallas?

104 Who were the first three players to have three-touchdown games against Dallas in 1960?

105 Who had the longest kickoff return for Dallas in the Cowboys' first year?

106 Who was the first Cowboy to have a two-touchdown game?

107 Who was the first Cowboy to score on an 80-yard reception?

108 Who had the first 50-yard field goal for the Cowboys?

109 His 27-yard field goal provided the winning points in Dallas' first regular-season victory.

113 Who was the leading scorer in that first win?

114 When did Dallas first post a break-even record?

115 What year did Roger Staubach get his first start for Dallas?

116 Why did he start?

117 Who was the first Cowboys quarterback to throw for 2,500 yards in one season — and when did he do it?

118 Who was the first player from Elizabeth City State to play for Dallas?

119 Who was the first Cowboy to total 10,000 yards combined rushing and receiving?

120 Name the first Cowboy to make the cover of "Newsweek."

121 Who was the first rookie to lead the Cowboys in scoring?

122 He was the first Cowboy quarterback to be selected for the Pro Bowl.

DALLAS COWBOYS TRIVIA 80 CHALLENGE CONTEST!

Who was the first Cowboy to rush for more than 1,500 yards in one season?

A. Calvin Hill. **B.** Walt Garrison. **C.** Tony Dorsett. **D.** Don Perkins.

110 He caught a 17-yard pass to tie the game before the field goal.

111 Who caught Don Meredith's first touchdown pass for Dallas?

112 In the Cowboys' first victory, he scored the first touchdown on a 44-yard reception.

123 When were the Cowboys first "perfect" in pre-season?

124 Name the Cowboys' first college draft choice.

125 What was the first year in which the Cowboys began the regular season with eight victories?

126 When was the last time Dallas started 8-0?

127 Which team broke that first eight-game winning streak?

128 What happened after Dallas had the first eight-game streak broken?

129 What team ended the second 8-0 start?

130 Which was the first NFC Championship game without an interception?

131 Who won the last Playoff Bowl?

132 When did Roger Staubach retire?

133 What were Joe Bob Isbell and Dale Memmelaar known for?

The last time Roger Staubach had to answer to the press as a member of the Cowboys.

DALLAS COWBOYS TRIVIA **81** CHALLENGE CONTEST!

Who was the first No. 1 pick by the Cowboys who was also the NFL's No. 1 draft pick?

A. Bob Lilly. **B.** Danny White. **C.** Ed (Too Tall) Jones. **D.** Tony Dorsett.

DALLAS COWBOYS TRIVIA **82** **CHALLENGE CONTEST!**

Who was the first former Olympian to play for Dallas?

A. Bob Hayes. **B.** Colin Ridgway. **C.** Mel Renfro. **D.** Amos Marsh.

---

134 What year did the Cowboys win their first division title?

135 Who was the first Cowboy to run for more than 5,000 career yards?

136 Who was the first Cowboys quarterback on a Topps bubble game card?

137 What was the first year of the Oak Farms Dairies' Favorite Cowboy contest?

138 What was the first year in which Tony Dorsett failed to rush for 1,000 yards since high school?

139 Name the Cowboy who was the first collegiate back to rush for at least 1,000 yards in four straight seasons.

140 Who was the first Cowboy to have 10 interceptions in one year?

141 What was the first American Football League team the Cowboys played in a regular-season game?

142 What was the score in that game?

143 When did Dallas first play in the Hall of Fame game?

DALLAS COWBOYS TRIVIA **83** **CHALLENGE CONTEST!**

Who was the first Cowboy draft choice from the Southwest Conference?

A. Don Talbert. **B.** Sonny Davis. **C.** Bob Lilly. **D.** E.J. Holub.

(FIRST AND LAST — ANSWERS)

A

1 Herb Scott, Pat Donovan, and Bob Breunig.

2 He lost nine yards.

3 White — it was tipped back to him.

4 The Cowboys, 37-13, over Baltimore.

5 On a 38-yard interception return against the New York Giants.

6 On a fumble recovery in 1979.

7 He threw a 12-yard touchdown pass to Billy Joe DuPree.

8 He recovered a fumble in the end zone against Philadelphia in 1980.

9 Herb Scott, who drew a penalty, in a playoff game against the Rams.

10 Tony Hill.

11 He went three for 10 — in the Pro Bowl.

12 Duane Thomas.

13 Ron Springs.

14 Rod Hill.

15 Detroit.

16 John Jacobs (a free agent signed in 1963).

17 Washington.

uane Thomas: Is that a smile?

Robert Shaw: the first draft pick during Roger Staubach's last year.

18 Eddie LeBaron.

19 Johnny Unitas.

20 Lenny Moore.

21 Robert Shaw.

22 In 1969.

23 Danny Villanueva.

24 Mel Renfro in 1964.

25 Cleveland.

26 In 1964.

27 St. Louis and New York.

28 Michael Downs (with seven).

29 In 1963 they were 3-2.

30 Dan Reeves (and he still holds the single-season touchdown record — 16 — for the Cowboys).

31 Robert Newhouse in 1976.

32 In 1963.

33 Harold Hays.

34 Ron Springs.

35 In a flag football game during the 1985 Cowboys Reunion.

36 D.D. Lewis — 1981 was his last season.

37 Michael Downs.

38 He ran for an 84-yard touchdown against Philadelphia.

39 Yes, the first and only. Calvin Hill is closest to the mark among other running backs with a 153-yard effort.

40 No, but he scored twice in his second game.

41 That was the day the first game was played in Texas Stadium.

42 He was the Most Valuable Player in the Playoff Bowl win over Minnesota.

43 He was benched for ineffectiveness in a 31-20 loss to Cleveland.

44 Walt Kowalczyk (91 yards vs. Los Angeles).

45 Dick Bielski on a 17-yard pass from Eddie LeBaron.

46 In his first year, 1961, against Minnesota (108 yards).

47 Jerry Norton returned a blocked field goal 94 yards for a touchdown against St. Louis.

48 Amos Marsh's 101-yard kickoff return vs. Philadelphia in 1962.

49 Frank Clarke with a 1,043-yard effort in 1962. He's not listed as Dallas' leading receiver that year because Billy Howton had more catches.

50 In 1964, for one game while Jerry Tubbs was sidelined with an injury.

51 St. Louis, in his fourth game as a professional.

52 Frank Clarke. He and Jerry Tubbs both played through 1967 but Tubbs had retired once before.

53 Jim Colvin.

54 Dickie Daniels.

55 Rafael Septien.

56 He suffered a torn thigh muscle in pre-season and missed most of the regular season.

57 Yes, on a 45-yard pass reception.

58 He scored on an 11-yard run.

59 Don Perkins in 1961.

60 Frank Clarke, with 241 against Washington in 1962.

61 Lee Roy Jordan and Ralph Neely.

62 David McDaniels in 1968.

63 John Niland.

64 Chuck Howley with six in 1968.

65 Mike Clark in 1968 and '69.

66 Mike Clark.

67 Amos Marsh vs. Washington in 1962.

68 Calvin Hill.

69 Tody Smith.

70 In 1975 (so was the second).

71 Aaron Kyle.

72 Duane Thomas, Rayfield Wright, Ron Widby, and Roger Staubach.

73 Walt Garrison.

74 Yes, in 1972.

75 Blaine Nye, Drew Pearson, and Cliff Harris.

76 Efren Herrera.

77 Frank Clarke.

78 In the Cowboys' first game.

79 Philadelphia (in Dallas' second game).

80 Frank Clarke.

81 Don McIlhenny.

82 Forty-five (he was the leading rusher).

83 Bullocks (77 yards). Marsh had a 70-yarder.

84 All went for touchdowns.

85 Both were intercepted.

86 Jim Cooper.

87 Jim Cooper.

88 Doug Dennison.

89 Randy White and Efren Herrera.

90 Tony Hill.

91 Lynn Hoyem.

92 In 1980; they also did it in 1981.

93 They were 97, 79, and 68 yards.

94 Scott Laidlaw and Robert Newhouse.

95 The New York Jets.

96 Robert Shaw.

97 Tony Dorsett.

98 St. Louis, 37-31, in 1975.

99 Washington, 30-24, also in 1975.

100 Rafael Septien. He started the string in 1978 and is still going as the leader each year.

101 The New York Giants.

102 Ed (Too Tall) Jones and John Dutton.

103 He threw for 75-yard and 53-yard touchdown passes and ran for a three-yard TD in a 24-3 victory over St. Louis.

104 Jim Taylor of Green Bay, Raymond Berry of Baltimore, and Bobby Mitchell of Cleveland.

105 Bill Butler, 60 yards.

106 Jim Doran (in Dallas' first game).

107 Frank Clarke.

108 Sam Baker, a 53-yarder in 1962.

109 Allen Green.

110 Dick Bielski.

111 Walt Kowalczyk.

112 Frank Clarke.

113 Allen Green.

114 In 1965, the Cowboys had a 7-7 record.

115 In 1969.

116 Craig Morton dislocated his finger.

117 Don Meredith in 1966.

118 Jethro Pugh.

119 Tony Dorsett (he passed the mark in 1983).

120 Thomas (Hollywood) Henderson.

121 Dick VanRaaphorst.

122 Eddie LeBaron.

123 In 1966 they were 5-0.

124 Bob Lilly.

125 In 1977.

126 In 1983.

127 The St. Louis Cardinals beat the Cowboys, 24-17.

Harold Hays, a special captain.

28 Dallas also lost the next week, to Pittsburgh, but then went on to win its next seven — including the Super Bowl over Denver.

29 The Los Angeles Raiders beat the Cowboys, 40-38. The Raiders, by the way, went on from there to become Super Bowl champions.

30 Dallas vs. Washington in 1972.

31 The Los Angeles Rams beat Dallas, 31-0.

32 Following the 1979 season (in March 1980).

33 The first Cowboy messenger guards.

134 In 1966.

135 Don Perkins.

136 Don Heinrich. Eddie LeBaron was on a card before Heinrich but not as a Cowboy.

137 In 1968.

138 In 1980 — the year of the strike.

139 Tony Dorsett.

140 Mel Renfro.

141 The Kansas City Chiefs (in 1970).

142 Dallas won, 27-16.

143 In 1968; Chicago was the opponent.

THE ONE AND ONLY

From Jerry Tubbs and L.G. Dupre to Everson Walls and James Jones . . . th
Cowboys have written their record book. Tony Dorsett, Roger Staubach, an
Charlie Waters are some of the names that keep popping up in the book an
on annual lists of leaders. But those three have plenty of company.

Q

1 In what season did Danny White break Roger Staubach's record for most touchdown passes in a single season?

2 He once held the NFL record for most catches by a tight end in a single season with 75.

3 Which four Cowboy passing records did Danny White break in 1983?

4 Who held the records?

5 What record did Ron Springs break in 1983?

6 Who had a better average per rushing attempt, Tony Dorsett or Roger Staubach?

7 Which three players were with the Cowboys for their first two appearances in the Hall of Fame game?

8 What special play did Ike Thomas duplicate in back-to-back games in 1971?

9 Who broke Don Perkins' reign as the team's leading rusher in 1965 with 757 yards?

10 He's the Cowboys all-time interception leader.

11 What categories did Duane Thomas lead the Cowboys in during the 1970 season?

12 Who was Dallas' leading ground-gaining running back in 1976?

Tony Hill

13 What year did Robert Newhouse lea
the team in rushing?

14 Who held the record for most catch
by a tight end until Billy Joe DuPr
broke it in 1976 with 42?

15 He led the team in receiving fo
times during an 11-year career ar
averaged better than eight yards p
carry as a runner.

164

6 In both 1974 and '76 he scored touchdowns by recovering fumbles in the end zone.

7 He's the Cowboys' all-time leading receiver with 489 catches.

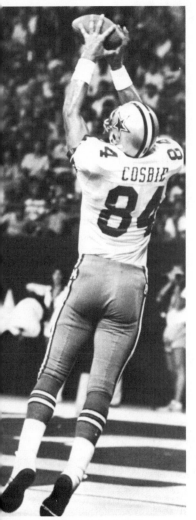

'Ds were his specialty in 1981.

18 He ran for more than 700 yards in 1977 but finished second on the team.

19 He closed out his career in 1977 with two interceptions, running his Cowboys total past 50.

20 He led the team in interceptions in 1977 with five.

21 What was Tony Dorsett's longest scoring play during his second season?

22 He had more than 400 yards in punt returns and more than 600 in kickoff runbacks in 1978 to lead the club in each category for the third year in a row.

23 He led Dallas in receiving yards in 1978 with 823.

24 Who led the Cowboys in interceptions in 1960 and how many did he have?

25 In 1961 he set the Cowboys record for most receptions in a game (11) that stood until 1967.

26 As a rookie he set the team record for longest run from scrimmage (71 yards) that lasted one year.

27 He boomed a 75-yard punt for Dallas in 1962, a record that lasted for eight years.

28 He had 38 kickoff returns for 780 yards in 1979, the most yardage since Dennis Morgan's 823 in 1974.

29 Who broke Butch Johnson's three-year hold on the punt return leadership in 1979?

30 Who played more games at center than any other player in Cowboys history?

31 Who broke Butch Johnson's records for punt returns and punt return yardage in 1980?

32 His 22.5-yard kickoff return average in 1980 was the best since Butch Johnson's 24.4-yard mark in 1977.

33 When did Drew Pearson catch his 366th pass, to move ahead of Bob Hayes as the Cowboys' all-time leading receiver?

DALLAS COWBOYS TRIVIA **84** **CHALLENGE CONTEST!**

He tied a two-year record set in 1971-72 by Bill Bradley by leading the league in interceptions both seasons.

A. Mel Renfro. **B.** Charlie Waters. **C.** Everson Walls. **D.** Michael Downs.

---

34 When did Tony Dorsett pass Robert Newhouse on the Cowboys' all-time rushing list (for third place)?

35 Who else did Tony Dorsett pass on the all-time rushing list that year?

36 Amos Bullocks set the record for the longest run from scrimmage in 1962 with a 73-yarder. How many times has Tony Dorsett surpassed that standard?

37 Who led the Cowboys in tackles from 1977 through '81?

38 He ranked only seventh on the club in receiving in 1981, but tied Butch Johnson in TD catches with five.

39 How many 100-yard receiving games did Drew Pearson have?

40 He fell one short of Preston Pearson's record for catches by a running back with 46 in 1981.

41 His 11 receptions against New England in 1981 was a team record for most catches by a running back.

42 How long did it take Everson Walls to rank among Dallas' top 10 career interception leaders?

43 How many times did Everson Walls

intercept two passes in a game in h first two seasons?

44 This rookie led the team in kicko returns and punt returns in 1963.

45 He caught only six passes in his fir four games in 1964, but still set a tea record with 65 receptions.

46 How long did the record stand?

47 He led the team — or shared the lea — in quarterback traps for 10 straig seasons, beginning in 1973.

48 Who broke his lead in 1983?

49 What was the most rushing yar gained in a season by Don Perkins?

50 Who led the Cowboys in rushing 1960?

51 Who led the team in scoring th year?

52 He holds the club record with 99 co secutive PATs.

53 He played in 196 consecutive games, Cowboy record.

54 In what year and against which opp nent did Billy Joe DuPree have h first three-touchdown game?

55 In 1973 he intercepted three passes

DALLAS COWBOYS TRIVIA **85** **CHALLENGE CONTEST!**

Who were the only Cowboys to play in all three decades?

A. Roger Staubach and Bob Hayes.   **B.** D.D. Lewis and Larry Cole
C. Rayfield Wright and Pettis Norman. **D.** Charlie Waters and Cliff Harris

---

DALLAS COWBOYS TRIVIA **86** CHALLENGE CONTEST!

How many times did Roger Staubach bring the Cowboys to victory when they were behind in the fourth quarter?

A. Twenty-three times.　　**B.** Nineteen.　　**C.** Thirty-one.　　**D.** Thirteen.

three consecutive Cincinnati Bengals possessions in a 38-10 Cowboys win.

6 What touchdown distance record did Eddie LeBaron set in 1962 that lasted four years?

7 Whose record did he break?

8 Who broke Tony Dorsett's record of 11 straight years of rushing for 1,000 yards or more?

9 Who holds the team record for most consecutive playoff passes without

throwing an interception?

60 Who had more rushing yards in his Cowboys career, Roger Staubach or Dan Reeves?

61 Who had more career interceptions, Lee Roy Jordan or Cliff Harris?

62 Did Danny White have more yards passing or punting in 1981?

63 In eight seasons with Dallas, how many times was Don Perkins the team rushing leader?

DALLAS COWBOYS TRIVIA **87** CHALLENGE CONTEST!

How many times did Roger Staubach bring the Cowboys back to victory when the Cowboys were losing in the final two minutes?

A. Nine times.　　**B.** Eleven.　　**C.** Fourteen.　　**D.** Nineteen.

arry Cole, a study in longevity.

(THE ONE AND ONLY — ANSWERS)

1 In 1980 (his first) when he threw for 28.

2 Mike Ditka (though he never quite matched those numbers at Dallas).

3 Most attempts, completions, yards, and touchdowns in a single season.

4 Roger Staubach held the first three; White held the other.

5 The record for most catches in one year; he caught 73 to break Frank Clarke's record of 65.

6 Staubach averaged 5.5; Dorsett is just over 4.5.

7 Larry Cole, D.D. Lewis, and Rayfield Wright.

8 He returned kickoffs for touchdowns.

9 Dan Reeves.

10 Mel Renfro (with 52).

11 Rushing and kickoff returns.

12 Doug Dennison with 542 yards.

13 In 1975 with 930 yards.

14 Mike Ditka (30 in 1972).

15 Drew Pearson.

16 Drew Pearson.

17 Drew Pearson.

18 Robert Newhouse.

19 Mel Renfro.

20 Cliff Harris.

21 A 91-yard reception against the Baltimore Colts.

22 Butch Johnson.

23 Tony Hill.

24 Don Bishop with three.

25 Billy Howton.

26 Amos Marsh.

27 Sam Baker.

28 Ron Springs.

29 Steve Wilson.

30 John Fitzgerald.

31 James Jones.

32 James Jones.

33 Against St. Louis in 1980.

34 In the first game of 1981.

35 Calvin Hill (for second place) and Don Perkins (to take over the No. 1 spot).

36 Five.

37 Bob Breunig.

38 Doug Cosbie.

39 Eighteen.

40 Ron Springs.

41 Ron Springs.

42 Two years (25 games).

43 Five times.

44 Jim Stiger.

45 Frank Clarke.

46 Until 1983, when Ron Springs broke with 73.

47 Harvey Martin.

48 Randy White.

49 He had 945 in 1962.

50 L.G. Dupre with 362 yards.

51 Fred Cone, who scored 39 points.

52 Mike Clark (he set the record over three-year period).

53 Bob Lilly.

54 In 1973 DuPree had three against Louis.

55 Lee Roy Jordan.

56 The longest pass play, an 85-yarder to Amos Marsh.

57 His own record of 80 yards set in 1961.

58 The NFL Players Association by calling a strike.

59 Roger Staubach.

60 Staubach (2,264 to 1,990).

61 Jordan had 32; Harris had 29.

62 Punting, 3,284; he had 3,098 passing.

63 Seven.

Harvey Martin, setting the trap.

THE ALL-TIME TEAM

In 1984, the Dallas Cowboys asked their fans to vote for the all-time team – and as part of the 25th anniversary celebration, the Silver Season All-Time Team was announced.

Seven players who were active in 1984 were included on the 27-man squad. And 18 of the 27 were active during the 1974 season.

Here are the players selected:

OFFENSE

Player	Pos.	No.	Years Played
Roger Staubach	QB	12	1969-79
Don Meredith	QB	17	1960-68
Tony Dorsett	RB	33	1977-85*
Walt Garrison	RB	32	1966-74
Don Perkins	RB	43	1961-68
Drew Pearson	WR	88	1973-83
Bob Hayes	WR	22	1965-74
Billy Joe DuPree	TE	89	1973-83
John Fitzgerald	C	62	1971-80
John Niland	G	76	1966-74
Herb Scott	G	68	1975-84
Rayfield Wright	T	70	1967-79
Ralph Neely	T	73	1965-77
Danny White	P	11	1976-85*
Rafael Septien	K	1	1978-85*

DEFENSE

Player	Pos.	No.	Years Played
Bob Lilly	DT	74	1961-74
Randy White	DT	54	1975-85*
Ed Jones	DE	72	1974-85*
Harvey Martin	DE	79	1973-83
Chuck Howley	LB	54	1961-72
Lee Roy Jordan	LB	55	1963-76
D.D. Lewis	LB	50	1968-81
Mel Renfro	CB	20	1964-77
Cornell Green	CB	34	1962-74
Everson Walls	CB	24	1981-85*
Charlie Waters	S	41	1970-81
Cliff Harris	S	43	1970-79

*— Still active.

THE BEST MAN

The Dallas Cowboys are in the National Football League record books for several team and individual accomplishments — and over the years have had numerous players among league statistical leaders.

1 Who was the first Cowboy to finish among the top 10 NFL receivers in a season?

2 Who was the first member of the Cowboys to rank among the top 10 in the NFL for rushing in a season?

3 In its first season, Dallas had two players rank in punting statistics in the NFL's top 10. Who were they?

4 In 1964, one Dallas Cowboys rookie was ranked in the NFL's top 10 in three categories. Who was he and what were the categories?

5 Which three teams shared the record for most consecutive playoff appearances (eight) before the Cowboys broke the record in 1983?

6 He ranks in the all-time top five in playoff receptions.

7 His 89-yard return is the second-best kickoff runback in NFL playoff history.

8 He was No. 4 in the NFC in punt returns in 1980, the highest rank for a

A man who saw double duty.

DALLAS COWBOYS TRIVIA **88** CHALLENGE CONTEST!

In 1964, another Cowboy rookie was among the top 20 in two categories. Who was he and what were his two categories?

A. Bob Hayes, receiving and scoring. **B.** Dick VanRaaphorst, field goals and scoring. **C.** Don Perkins, rushing and scoring. **D.** Billy Lothridge, punting and receiving.

Cowboy since another rookie was fourth four years earlier.

9 He was ranked in the top 10 in both the NFC and NFL in 1980. Who was he and what were the categories?

10 Where did Tony Dorsett finish in NFL rushing in his Cowboy record-setting fifth season, 1981?

11 In 1981, Dallas had two NFL leaders. Who were they?

12 This former Cowboy was the second-ranked NFL quarterback in 1981. His best standing with Dallas was fifth in the NFL.

13 He led the NFL tight ends with nine touchdown receptions in 1978.

14 He was the NFC's No. 2 scorer in 1978.

15 He had the best game in the league as a receiver in 1979 with 213 yards.

16 This SMU ex led the league in interceptions and punting at St. Louis before coming to the Cowboys in a trade in 1962.

17 In his first year with the Cowboys, this kicker was ranked in three categories in the NFL's top 10. Who was he and what were the categories?

18 Which two Cowboys ranked in the top 10 in the NFC in two categories each in 1981?

Walt Garrison, a cowboy's Cowboy.

Tony Dorsett gets started on an NFL record-setting run.

19 Among non-kickers, he ranked among the NFC's top 10 scorers in 1981.

20 Who were the first two players in NFL history to gain 1,000 yards in each of their first three seasons.

21 He holds the NFL playoff-game record for field-goal accuracy.

22 Which two Cowboys rank among the NFL's all-time playoff leaders in number of field goals?

23 The only member of the Cowboys from Chattanooga University tied for second in the NFL in punt returns his only year.

24 This same player was tied for the league lead in total returns that year. How many did he return?

25 In 1962, Dallas had two players ranked among the NFL's top 10 scorers for the first time. Who were they?

26 This Cowboy holds the NFL record for the longest run from scrimmage, a record he set in 1982's strike-shortened season. Who made the run and how long was it?

27 Against what team did a Cowboys player set an NFL record for longest run from scrimmage?

28 What were the results of the game when a Cowboy set a league record for longest run from scrimmage?

29 He led the Cowboys and the NFL in scoring in 1981.

30 Which Cowboy broke Don Hutson's all-time receiving record?

DALLAS COWBOYS TRIVIA **89** **CHALLENGE CONTEST!**

Which Cowboy participated in an NFL-record 27 playoff games?

A. Charlie Waters.   **B.** Mel Renfro.   **C.** D.D. Lewis.   **D.** Larry Cole.

31 How many times did Roger Staubach lead the league in passing?

32 Dallas had the best record of any NFC team against AFC teams in the 1970s. Only one season did the Cowboys have a losing record against the AFC. What was the year and the record?

33 What two Cowboys were ranked in the NFL's top 10 in punt returns in 1969?

34 In 1981, this Cowboys defensive back led the NFL in interceptions with 11.

35 Tony Dorsett set an NCAA record for most yards gained against one opponent in a career with 754 yards. Who was the opponent?

36 This lineman set a Super Bowl record with a 27-yard sack of Bob Griese.

37 Who held the record that a Cowboy runner broke in 1982 for longest run from scrimmage in the NFL?

Bob Lilly

DALLAS COWBOYS TRIVIA **90** **CHALLENGE CONTEST!**

Tony Dorsett rushed for 1,646 yards in 1981, but lost the NFL rushing title by less than 30 yards. Who beat him?

A. Walter Payton.   **B.** Earl Campbell.   **C.** George Rogers.
D. Chuck Foreman.

---

38 In what year did Tony Dorsett win his first NFC rushing title?

39 What was unusual about Tony Dorsett's first NFC rushing title?

40 He was the first Cowboy to lead the NFL in an offensive category.

41 He was second in the NFC in receiving in his second season (1974).

42 He led the Cowboys and was fourth in the NFC in both kickoff and punt returns in 1971.

43 He led the team and was in the NFC's top 10 in catches in 1971.

44 Roger Staubach led the NFC in passing in both 1971 and '73. How did he rank in overall statistics in the NFL?

45 Though he failed to rank in average per return, he had more yards than any of the top 10 kickoff returners in the NFL in 1974.

46 He led the NFC and NFL in field goals in 1976.

47 This kick return specialist had more than 1,100 yards in his only season in Dallas.

48 He averaged 12.4 yards per punt return in 1977, the most among NFC players with 10 or more runbacks.

49 He led the team and was in the top 10 in the NFC in kickoff and punt returns in 1977.

50 He became only the sixth free-agent rookie to play in the Pro Bowl.

174

51 How many years did it take Tony Dorsett to gain a place among the NFL's all-time top 10 rushers?

52 Which two Cowboys were ranked among the NFL's top 10 rushers in 1966?

53 One of the Cowboys ranked in the NFL top 10 rushers in 1966 was ranked among the top 10 scorers. Who was it?

54 This future Cowboy led the league in kickoff returns in 1968.

55 He failed to lead the team in quarter-back traps in his final year but still finished with a career total of 125.

56 How many PATs did Rafael Septien kick in 1980 to set the NFC record?

57 He was No. 2 in the NFL in interceptions and return yardage in 1961.

58 The Cowboys finally had a receiver among the NFL leaders in 1964, the No. 3 pass catcher. Who was he?

59 This future Cowboy was the No. 2 receiver in the NFL in 1964.

60 How many seasons as a pro has Tony Dorsett failed to rush for 1,000 yards?

DALLAS COWBOYS TRIVIA **91** **CHALLENGE CONTEST!**

He was the first Cowboy to lead the league in a defensive category.

A. Everson Walls. **B.** Lee Roy Jordan. **C.** Mel Renfro. **D.** Chuck Howley.

(THE BEST MAN — ANSWERS)

1 Billy Howton, who was sixth in 1961 with 56 catches.

2 Don Perkins had 815 yards for sixth place in 1961.

3 Dave Sherer was the No. 7 punter in the league with a 42.5 average. Bill Butler's 10.1 average on 13 punt returns ranked him No. 2 in that category.

4 Mel Renfro. He was No. 3 in punt returns, No. 4 in interceptions and No. 7 in kickoff returns.

5 Los Angeles (1973-80), Pittsburgh (1972-79), and Dallas (1966-73).

6 Drew Pearson.

7 Rod Hill (he did it against Green Bay on January 9, 1983).

8 James Jones (with a 10.1 average).

9 Danny White. He was seventh in the NFC and ninth in the NFL in passing, and fifth in the NFC and 10th in the NFL in punting.

10 Second. Dorsett had 1,646 yards, averaging 107 yards in the first 15 games that year — but was held to 39 yards in the season finale by the New York Giants.

11 Rafael Septien was tied for No. 1 in scoring with 112 points. Rookie Everson Walls led the league in interceptions with 11.

12 Craig Morton of Denver.

13 Billy Joe DuPree.

14 Rafael Septien with 94 points. The previous year, Efren Herrera ranked No. 2 with 93.

15 Tony Hill (against Philadelphia).

16 Jerry Norton.

17 Sam Baker was No. 3 in punting and field goals and No. 6 in scoring.

18 Danny White (in punting and passing) and Rafael Septien (in scoring and field goals).

19 Ron Springs (he was sixth with 72 points).

20 Tony Dorsett and John Brockington.

21 Rafael Septien (18 of 21 — including 18 of 20 for Dallas).

22 Rafael Septien is third and Toni Fritsch second (behind George Blanda's all-time record of 22).

23 Bill Butler with a 10.1 average in 1960.

24 Thirteen, including a long return of 46 yards.

25 Sam Baker was sixth with 92 points and Frank Clarke ranked seventh with 84 points on 14 touchdowns.

26 Tony Dorsett, who scored on a 99-yard run.

Rafael Septien, with Dennis Thurman.

27 Tony Dorsett's 99-yard run came against Minnesota in the last game of the 1982 season.

28 Dallas was defeated by Minnesota, 31-27.

29 Rafael Septien.

30 Billy Howton.

31 Four times — 1971, 1973, 1978, and 1979.

32 The year was 1979 and the record was 1-3.

33 Bob Hayes and Mel Renfro.

34 Everson Walls.

35 Notre Dame.

36 Bob Lilly.

37 Andy Uram of Green Bay set the record of 97 yards in 1939.

38 1982.

39 It was the first year in which Dorsett failed to rush for 1,000 yards as a pro during the regular season. In the strike-shortened season, Dorsett had 745 yards in the nine regular-season games.

40 Roger Staubach.

41 Drew Pearson.

42 Cliff Harris.

43 Walt Garrison.

44 First both years.

45 Dennis Morgan (823 yards).

46 Efren Herrera.

47 Dennis Morgan.

48 Tony Hill.

49 Butch Johnson.

50 Everson Walls.

51 He entered the NFL's top 10 career rushers in his seventh year.

52 Dan Reeves (sixth) and Don Perkins (seventh).

53 Reeves was tied for sixth. Another

Tony Hill

Cowboy, Danny Villanueva, was second.

54 Preston Pearson.

55 Harvey Martin.

56 Septien kicked 59, a record later broken by Mark Moseley.

57 Don Bishop.

58 Frank Clarke, with 65 catches for 973 yards.

59 Mike Ditka.

60 None, technically ... in 1982 he actually failed to reach 1,000 yards during the regular season, but had 266 yards in the playoffs for a total of 1,011 yards for all 12 games.

TAKING CARE OF BUSINESS

Several Cowboys have had other sports careers or gotten into other lines of work during or after their careers with Dallas. Don Meredith left Dallas and later became a part of ABC's "Monday Night Football" telecasts, but not all the post-career ventures have earned as much attention for Cowboys.

Q

1 This former Cowboy, also a former SMU Mustang, is a licensed florist.

2 These five players were owners of Dynamic Dave, the son of 1975 Kentucky Derby winner Cannonade.

3 He had two sports careers — and was once selected in the NBA draft by the San Antonio Spurs.

4 This defensive back later became the youngest full professor at Syracuse University.

5 What was the original name of Harvey Martin's barbecue restaurants?

6 Who purchased 200 tickets for Ed (Too Tall) Jones' Dallas ring debut and distributed them to the Cowboys?

7 In 1979, Charlie Waters was injured but he had another job with the Cowboys later in the season. What was it?

8 He talked to the Texas Rangers about switching to a baseball career.

9 Who originated the Cowboy Bandanas?

10 Why was Ed (Too Tall) Jones' bout in Tucson, Arizona, against Allan Johnson called off?

11 Which two players signed with Birmingham of the World Football League but never played there because the team folded?

12 This former defensive back went on to become director of scouting for Washington.

13 He was once the baseball property of the St. Louis Browns.

14 This member of the staff held one of the few scoring records (30 points in one half) that Wilt Chamberlain failed to break during his Kansas basketball career.

15 This former Cowboy has been heard extolling the virtues of an insurance company that specializes in "insurance for Texans."

Jethro Pugh

DALLAS COWBOYS TRIVIA **92** **CHALLENGE CONTEST!**

They opened a football camp for kids in the late 1960s.

A. Tom Landry and Gil Brandt. **B.** Don Perkins and Don Meredith.
C. George Andrie and Bob Lilly. **D.** Roger Staubach and Craig Morton.

16 He played professional basketball and coached five years at Kansas.

17 This former staff member was the athletic trainer when the Air Force Academy opened in 1955.

18 Who played two years for Toledo in the United Football League before joining the Cowboys?

19 He was an All-Academic selection as a math major at Rice in the 1960s.

20 He was an All-City basketball player at South Oak Cliff High School in Dallas.

21 His father was Attorney General of Alabama.

22 He was the second collegiate All-American basketball player to play for the Cowboys.

23 He was a member of the Confederate Air Force.

24 Who won the American Football Coaches Association golf tournament in Dallas in 1980?

25 He founded the Hoopsters.

26 He worked in the sports department of KDFW-TV during the off-season.

27 Who was Colorado's heavyweight boxing champion in 1978?

28 What was Drew Pearson's connection with Southwest Conference basketball?

29 What was his connection with the Distilled Spirits Council?

30 Who sponsored the Fellowship of Christian Athletes Open golf tournament at Royal Oaks in Dallas in the 1970s and '80s?

31 This one-time receiver worked out with a Dallas trainer and considered a career in boxing.

32 Which two Dallas area sports stars played together on the infield at Arizona State in the early 1970s?

33 As a trackman, this All-Pro cornerback ran a 9.5 100-yard dash.

34 He was a three-year letterman at Illinois in basketball.

35 He was the second former Michigan State basketball player to work at tight end for the Cowboys.

36 Who was the first?

Ron Widby

Walt Garrison, left, and Dave Manders.

37 What ended Walt Garrison's football career?

38 Who was the former Seattle basketball forward who turned down a chance to play pro basketball in France?

39 He worked as a counselor at Spruce High School in 1976.

40 Who served as a judge in the Miss Oklahoma Pageant in 1977?

41 He once played for the Jets and Stags.

42 Who was the first collegiate track star to sign with the Cowboys?

43 Before joining the Cowboys, he was an outstanding sprinter at Oregon State.

44 He worked for NBC's "Survival of the Fittest" competition in New Zealand in 1982.

45 Which two former Cowboys were featured together in a Lite Beer commercial?

46 This quarterback's hobby was rattlesnake hunting.

47 Which two Cowboy backs signed contracts with the World Football League before the start of the 1974 season?

48 Why didn't Danny White join the Cowboys after they drafted him?

49 Who was the first Cowboy to make the transition from rodeo cowboy to football Cowboy?

50 What linebacker was an art teacher and Golden Gloves boxer before becoming a Cowboy?

DALLAS COWBOYS TRIVIA **93** **CHALLENGE CONTEST!**

What player was an All-American basketball player at Utah State?

A. Pete Gent. **B.** Cornell Green. **C.** Ed (Too Tall) Jones. **D.** John Dutton.

51 This former Cowboy, who later made a name for himself in another profession, worked for Tracy-Locke as an account executive.

52 He was featured with the Dallas Cowboys in a special Marvel comic book, "Danger in Dallas," in 1983.

53 When were the Cowboys sold?

54 What Cowboy was a professional in two other sports?

55 He had a string of men's clothing stores called "22 Shops."

56 Where did Calvin Hill enroll during his first off-season?

57 With which law firm did Dallas offer Eddie LeBaron a job when the Cowboys were negotiating with him in 1960?

58 What was Eddie LeBaron's earliest connection with Glenn Carano?

59 This Cowboy later became chaplain at Stephen F. Austin State University.

60 Who did Jerry Tubbs and Mike Falls work for during the off-season?

61 Who was Jerry Tubbs planning to work for before he was drafted by the Cowboys from another team?

62 He ran for a place on the Bedford City Council in 1973.

63 He was the proprietor of a Dallas restaurant-lounge called The Handlebar.

64 This Cowboy was a student of marine biology, with a specialty in shark behavioral research.

65 Which ex-Cowboy did an American Express commercial at a zoo?

66 He formed a novelty merchandising firm, promoting several Cowboys-related items.

67 He was a commentator for ABC on the 1980 "Super Teams" competition.

68 All-Pro linemen at their regular jobs, these Cowboys were spokesmen for Bridgeport's Runaway Bay during the 1960s and '70s.

69 This Cowboy was featured wearing underwear and pads in a Chap Stick advertisement in the 1960s.

70 In the 1960s, this busy Cowboy was featured in NFL Official Training Table Food ads.

71 Who was the defensive back featured in the NFL Official Locker Room Products ads in 1972?

72 He owns his own lumber company.

73 During a 20-year stint with the Air Force, he won a bronze star.

74 What incident does Tom Landry say "did more to change my image than anything I've done since I got into the coaching business?"

75 Who changed careers at 28, but came back?

76 Who were Abdullah Muhammad and Yaqui Meneses?

77 Several Cowboys host golf tournaments. What celebrity sports event did Randy White host?

78 He was a partner in a Midland mud company.

79 These two players, starters at the same position, did a commercial together before Super Bowl VI, then played on opposite sides in the game.

DALLAS COWBOYS TRIVIA 94 CHALLENGE CONTEST!

What Cowboy was a pro basketball player in the ABA?

A. Ron Widby. **B.** Cornell Green. **C.** Pete Gent. **D.** Rayfield Wright.

(TAKING CARE OF BUSINESS — ANSWERS)

A

1 Anthony Dickerson.

2 Gary Hogeboom, Bill Bates, Jeff Rohrer, Mike Renfro, and Brian Baldinger.

3 Ed (Too Tall) Jones.

4 Jim Ridlon.

5 Smokey John's.

6 Ed (Too Tall) Jones.

7 He was analyst on Cowboys radio broadcasts.

8 Charlie Waters.

9 Preston Pearson.

10 Only 200 advance tickets were sold.

11 Jethro Pugh and Rayfield Wright.

12 Dickie Daniels.

13 Ray Mathews (a wide receiver from Clemson).

14 Equipment manager Jack Eskridge.

15 Don Meredith.

16 Jack Eskridge.

17 Clint Houy.

18 Dave Manders.

19 Malcolm Walker.

20 Malcolm Walker.

21 Richmond Flowers.

22 Ron Widby.

23 Mike Clark.

24 John Mackovic.

25 Drew Pearson.

26 Drew Pearson.

27 Bill Roe.

28 He worked as an analyst on SWC telecasts.

29 He was national spokesman.

30 Tom Landry.

31 Percy Howard.

32 Former Ranger Bump Wills and Cowboy Danny White.

33 Mel Renfro.

34 Preston Pearson.

35 Billy Joe DuPree.

36 Pete Gent.

37 A rodeo accident.

38 Ron Howard (a tight end in the mid-1970s).

39 Bill Gregory.

40 Thomas (Hollywood) Henderson.

41 Jack Eskridge (he played professional basketball for the Chicago Stags and Indianapolis Jets).

42 No, it wasn't Bob Hayes; it was Dick Howard of New Mexico, who failed to make the team.

Rayfield Wright

43 Amos Marsh.

44 Ken Locker.

45 D.D. Lewis and Charlie Waters.

46 Clint Longley.

47 Calvin Hill and Craig Morton.

48 He signed with the World Football League.

49 Defensive back Kyle McFarlane.

50 Gene Babb.

51 Pete Gent.

52 Spider Man.

53 Following the 1983 season.

54 Ron Widby — basketball and golf.

55 Bob Hayes.

56 Perkins Theological Seminary.

57 Wynne and Wynne.

58 LeBaron worked in the same law firm with Carano's father.

59 Mike Falls.

60 For the Cowboys (they did PR work).

61 Coca-Cola.

62 Larry Cole.

63 Dave Edwards.

64 Dave Stalls.

65 Mike Ditka.

66 Preston Pearson.

67 Harvey Martin.

68 George Andrie and Bob Lilly.

69 Bob Lilly.

70 Bob Lilly.

71 Mel Renfro.

72 Lee Roy Jordan.

73 Buck Buchanan.

74 His commercial for American Express.

75 Ed (Too Tall) Jones.

76 Jones' first two boxing opponents.

77 The Lake Texoma Celebrity Open Striped Bass Tournament.

78 Tony Dorsett.

79 Roger Staubach and Bob Griese.

Malcolm Walker

Billy Joe DuPree

JUST FOR THE FUN OF IT

Many facts about the Cowboys, by their nature, can't be categorized. Like so[me] draft choices, they don't compute. So those facts are just thrown together int[o a] grab-bag full of tricks and fun.

Larry Cole closes in on New York's Joe Pisarcik.

1 Who was the All-Pro from Throckmorton, Texas?

2 What did Walt Garrison get instead of an automobile when he signed with the Cowboys?

3 What were the results of the Cowboys' overtime games in 1975?

4 Who was the receiver on Roger Staubach's storied "Hail Mary" pass?

5 Name the only four Cowboy players to play a full season at middle linebacker.

6 In 1973, what former Chicago Bear came to Dallas in a trade to become a backup quarterback?

7 This serviceman wrote Gil Brandt a letter from Vietnam asking for another football.

8 What was the result of the Cowboys' first meeting with the Denver Broncos during the 1977 season?

9 This player's 1962 Post cereal football card is one of the 20 hardest to get because it was printed on one of the less popular cereal boxes.

10 What was the significance of the 1973 Pro Bowl for the Cowboys?

11 Who is the well-known sideline cowboy at Texas Stadium?

12 Who were the original members of the NFC's Eastern Conference in 1973?

13 Who were the honorary captains for Dallas during the Silver Season?

14 What game did Mel Renfro single out as being the biggest in his career?

15 What was the Frito-Lay challenge?

16 What was Quadra?

17 Name four Cowboys who played high school football at Dallas South Oak Cliff.

18 What did punter Dave Sherer and Roger Staubach have in common?

19 Only two pro teams have posted longer winning season streaks than the Dallas Cowboys. Name them.

20 For how many consecutive seasons have the Cowboys had a .500 winning percentage or better?

21 What was the Cowboys' famous (or infamous) jinx of the '70s?

22 What did Tex Schramm do about the Cowboy "jinx"?

23 Who is Suzanne Mitchell?

24 How long did the Cowboys' winning streak last in 1982?

25 How many consecutive games did the Cowboys win following the 1982 players' strike?

26 Which was the first team to beat Dallas after the 1982 strike by NFL players?

27 What did Toni Fritsch do at the first NFL game he ever saw?

28 What kind of artificial surface covers the Texas Stadium playing field?

29 This Cowboy had 168 yards in kickoff returns in a game against Washington in 1964.

DALLAS COWBOYS TRIVIA **95** CHALLENGE CONTEST!

Against what team did Dan Reeves quarterback the Cowboys in 1971?

A. New York Giants. **B.** Philadelphia Eagles. **C.** Los Angeles Rams. **D.** St. Louis Cardinals.

30 He had a 100-yard interception return for a touchdown against San Francisco in 1965.

31 What was the Ralph Neely affair?

32 Who was missing from the play when Tony Dorsett ran 99 yards from scrimmage for a touchdown?

33 Who wins the Governor's Cup?

34 He was the tallest receiver to play for Dallas.

35 He caught four touchdown passes against Houston in 1970.

36 What did the Cowboys offer as "Pieces of Winning History" in the early 1980s?

37 Was there ever another Cowboys team in the NFL?

38 What was Walt Garrison's hobby?

39 He was featured on the 1979-80 Dallas Cowboys calendar.

40 This noted Cowboy personality was pictured in a striking Uncle Sam "I Want You" pose on pocket schedules for the 1985 season.

contests?

45 He was Jeff and Hazel's baby boy.

46 This former Cowboys defensive back was born on Christmas Day. He played for the Cowboys from 1970-78.

47 What is John Wooten's relationship with the Cowboys?

48 What is the focus of the annual "Life With the Cowboys" mailout?

49 What did Doug Donley call his doberman?

50 What is the Cowboys' NFL record for consecutive opening-game victories?

51 Tony Dorsett has scored touchdowns three ways in his pro career. What are they?

52 Ron Springs has accounted for touchdowns in what three ways?

53 In what ways has Danny White accounted for scores for the Cowboys?

54 When did Roger Staubach throw his first Hail Mary pass?

DALLAS COWBOYS TRIVIA **96** **CHALLENGE CONTEST!**

He succeeded Joe Theismann as quarterback at South River (N.J.) High School.

A. Charlie Waters. **B.** Glenn Carano. **C.** Gary Hogeboom.
D. Drew Pearson.

---

41 Who competed against his "childhood hero" when he came to the Cowboys in 1976?

42 Who were the offensive co-captains in 1981?

43 This game is commonly thought of as the one that pushed the Dallas Cowboys Cheerleaders into the national spotlight.

44 When Roger Staubach listed his 12 favorite games for "GameDay," how many of them were professional

55 What was pictured on the 1972 Cowboy media guide?

56 Who were the Cow Belles?

57 Who was older, Roger Staubach or Craig Morton?

58 What two Cowboy teammates who played the same position shared the same birthday?

59 Who did Glenn Carano beat out to become the Cowboys' No. 3 quarterback?

60 He was an All-Big 10 basketball player at Illinois.

61 These two former teammates — and former Super Bowl opponents — share the same birthday with baseball Hall of Famer Hank Aaron.

62 Did Bob Hayes spend his entire career with Dallas?

63 Trades involving quarterbacks made a difference in the Cowboys' 1975 draft. Explain how.

64 Who did Dallas have to give up to get Preston Pearson?

65 How did Dallas make room for Preston Pearson on the roster?

66 What was the first official act Preston Pearson had to perform when he arrived in Dallas?

67 Whose retirement gave Tom Rafferty a chance to start for the Cowboys — at right guard?

68 This player once showed up at a Pittsburgh airport with an orange tree.

69 Did Walt Garrison have a 1,000-yard season for Dallas?

70 Calvin Hill led the Cowboys in rushing in both 1972 and '73. Who led the team in receiving each year?

71 Did Calvin Hill pass Don Perkins on Dallas' all-time rushing list?

72 Who was the Cowboys' first draft pick from J.C. Smith College?

73 Name the three members of the Dirty Dozen who played just one season with Dallas.

74 He gained 24 yards on a kickoff return in 1977 — but didn't return a kickoff. Who was he and how did it happen?

75 Did Drew Pearson ever throw an incomplete pass for Dallas?

76 Who and what were featured on the 1979 media guide?

77 He was released after three preseason games in 1978 — but recalled when Dallas traded Golden Richards to Chicago.

78 For how many seasons did Pearson lead the Cowboys in receiving in the 1970s?

79 And how many times did Hill lead the team in the '70s in receiving?

80 These three players were all active in 1979 and at the time were among Dallas' top 10 career rushers.

81 Six players who were on the all-time top 10 receiving list were also active in 1979. Who were they?

82 Name the six players active in 1970 who are among Dallas' 10 all-time interception leaders.

83 How long did it take Tony Dorsett to become a 1,000-yard receiver for the Cowboys?

84 Dallas' longest run from scrimmage in 1960 was 34 yards. Who carried the ball?

DALLAS COWBOYS TRIVIA **97** **CHALLENGE CONTEST!**

After his Texas high school team won three straight state championships, he became an outstanding receiver for Don Meredith at SMU and later played for the Cowboys. Who was he and where did he go to high school?

A. Bob Hayes, Fort Worth Poly.
B. Glynn Gregory, Abilene High.
C. Lance Alworth, R.L. Turner.
D. Frank Clarke, Houston Madison.

85 In his first five years, how many times did Tony Dorsett have runs of 34 yards or more?

86 He set the Cowboy record with a 79-yard kickoff return in 1961 and broke it the next season. Who was he?

87 Does that record still stand?

88 Which three players had touchdown catches in Dallas' first victory?

89 In 1966, he had four straight games with a touchdown via the run.

90 Who caught Preston Pearson's 22-yard touchdown pass in 1981?

91 Who was the second Dallas quarterback, after Eddie LeBaron, to complete an 80-yard touchdown pass?

92 He was the second Cowboy to cover the distance of the field on a kickoff return.

93 Why were the Cowboys' attendance figures at home games listed as "estimated" for 1960 and '61?

94 Through Dallas' first five seasons, Cowboy running backs had eight 100-yard-plus games. Don Perkins had six 100-yard games. Who had the other two?

95 In college, he once completed a pass for a safety.

96 When Jethro Pugh retired, which two players became the senior members of the Cowboys?

97 Where did Dextor Clinkscale play in 1981?

98 Who was "the kid" who made Diron Talbert eat crow in 1974?

99 What film did Diron Talbert say the Redskins watched before each Dallas game to get psyched for the Cowboys?

100 Who was Nass Botha?

101 Why do Dallas Cowboy offensive linemen stand up — then go into their stance during the snap count?

102 Where did Tony Dorsett go to high school?

103 Name the opponent and the winner of the game at Texas Stadium when the 25th Anniversary Cowboys team was presented?

104 Which two players handled field goal and PAT chores for Dallas in 1961?

105 This Cowboy poet put it like this: "You gotta pay the cost if you wanna be the boss. Football is my bread and meat. If I don't catch, I don't eat." Who is this Cowboy poet laureate?

106 "I'm not going to score a lot of 60-yard TDs," said this Cowboy receiver. "If I can sneak past 'em once or twice a year, I'll be happy," he added. Who was the philosophical receiver?

107 One confident Cowboy pass-catcher described himself like this: "My strength is what I do after I catch the ball. I'm the best running receiver on the team and have been since I came to the Cowboys." Who said it?

108 Who did Tom Landry call "the miracle of the defensive team"?

109 How many yards did Tony Dorsett rush for in his first year at Dallas?

110 Did a big play help Tony Dorsett pass the 1,000-yard mark in the final

---

DALLAS COWBOYS TRIVIA **98** **CHALLENGE CONTEST!**

He participated in more games in the Cotton Bowl than any other Cowboy.

A. Don Meredith. **B.** Jerry Rhome. **C.** Roger Staubach. **D.** Sonny Gibbs.

DALLAS COWBOYS TRIVIA — 99 — CHALLENGE CONTEST!

He hitchhiked to Dallas during his sophomore year and made his first collegiate appearance in the annual OU-Texas game.

A. Lance Alworth. **B.** Lance Rentzel. **C.** Jerry Tubbs. **D.** Don Talbert.

game of his first year?

111 How many yards did Tony Dorsett gain in the fourth quarter of his first Super Bowl?

112 This member of the Dallas Cowboys organization spent several years as an entertainer in a resort in the Poconos.

113 What role did Paula Van Waggoner have with the Cowboys?

114 What did Roger Staubach claim was his goal when he came to the Cowboys?

115 In 1981, one Cowboy passed another for 15th place on the NFL's all-time rushing list. Who were they?

116 What was the "crowning touch" at Texas Stadium?

117 What was the special play Efren Herrera used from field goal formation?

118 In 1975, he joined the list of Cowboys "who didn't play college football" as a running back.

119 What former running back signed Preston Pearson to his first pro contract?

20 What does EPA mean to the Cowboys?

21 Name the three former Cowboy tackles selected to the Pro Football Hall of Fame's All-Pro team of the 1960s.

22 Which three Cowboys are on the All-Pro team of the 1970s?

23 Which Cowboy grew up in "Hell's Hole"?

124 What did "El Jardin" have to do with a Cowboy kicker?

125 Where did the Cowboys Cheerleaders tour in December 1979?

126 He speculated that the reason he received a second-place prize in the Oak Farms Dairies Favorite Cowboy contest in 1967 was because his hurriedly organized fan club had stuffed the ballot boxes.

127 What was the first year Butch Johnson asked to be traded?

128 When asked by "Playboy" who he would pick to quarterback his team, Roger Staubach or himself, who did Terry Bradshaw pick?

129 What year did the Cowboys originate their Spanish Network?

130 What station serves as the flagship station for the Spanish Network?

131 He was named president when a Dallas chapter of the NFL Alumni Association was formed in 1980.

132 Dallas has played only three teams in every year since it entered the National Football League. Name them.

133 What were the Cowboys' original colors?

134 He was president of the NFL Players Association in 1969.

135 Which two players were pictured on the Cowboys' 1961 media guide?

136 What was featured on the 1962 media guide?

137 What player was pictured on the 1963 media guide?

Hollywood Henderson shows off his dunk.

138 How did Amos Marsh score touchdowns in 1962?

139 He played fullback, guard, tackle, linebacker, center, and middle linebacker at SMU in the early 1960s before his tenure with Dallas.

140 Who was pictured on the 1965 media guide?

141 This receiver was featured on the cover of the 1966 media guide after an All-Pro and Pro Bowl year.

142 This Stanford ex was drafted by the Chiefs but signed with Dallas as a free agent in 1966.

143 This lineman was credited with two kickoff returns for a total of 18 yards in 1966.

144 Who was the Cowboys' second 100-yard rusher?

145 What did the judges rule in the Ralph Neely case?

146 He's pictured in a familiar pose on the cover of the 1967 media guide.

147 Who was pictured on the 1968 media guide, the year before he retired?

148 He is the Cowboys' all-time interception leader among linebackers.

149 How many quarterbacks rank among the Cowboys' top 10 career rushers?

150 Three players who were among the league's top six punters in 1968 were current or past Cowboys. Name them.

151 In 1961, Billy Howton was one of the NFL's top 10 receivers. Name four other players, past or future members of the Cowboys, who were also among the top 10.

152 Who was the only advertiser on Cowboys media guide in the 196' and what year did the ad appear?

53 What milestone did Lance Alworth pass in his first year with Dallas?

54 Which of the Cowboys' top two running backs among the 1971 draft picks lasted the longest?

55 When the Jacksonville Sharks folded in 1974, he joined the Cowboys as a regular on the punting team.

56 This kicker runs the Fighting Air Command museum in Denton.

57 What place on the Cowboys' all-time rushing list did Walt Garrison achieve before his retirement?

158 He set the club record for receptions by a running back with 46 in 1977 at the age of 32.

159 A basketball standout at Brigham Young, this 1973 draft choice didn't live up to the expectations like his brother did the year before.

160 What was Tom Landry's record against George Allen-coached Redskin teams?

DALLAS COWBOYS TRIVIA 100 CHALLENGE CONTEST!

He made a return appearance on the cover of the 1981 press guide, this time in a solo photo.

A. Randy White.   **B.** Mel Renfro.   **C.** Cliff Harris.   **D.** Calvin Hill.

(JUST FOR THE FUN OF IT — ANSWERS)

1 Bob Lilly.

2 A two-horse trailer.

3 They beat the Cardinals but lost to the Redskins.

4 Drew Pearson.

5 Jerry Tubbs, Lee Roy Jordan, Bob Breunig, and Eugene Lockhart.

6 Jack Concannon.

7 Roger Staubach.

8 Dallas won in the regular-season finale at Texas Stadium, 14-6.

9 Jerry Tubbs.

10 It was played in Texas Stadium.

11 Crazy Ray Jones.

12 Dallas, New York (Giants), St. Louis, Philadelphia, and Washington.

13 Former players.

14 The 1971 Pro Bowl, when he was named MVP.

15 Frito-Lay Inc. donated money to Boys Clubs of Dallas for points scored by the Cowboys.

16 The name of the scouting combine that included Dallas, the Los Angeles Rams, San Francisco, and new member New Orleans.

17 Malcolm Walker, Everson Walls, Harvey Martin, and Guy Reese.

18 Both played at New Mexico Military Institute.

19 The New York Yankees and the Montreal Canadiens.

20 Twenty-one.

21 The blue jerseys.

The Dallas Cowboys Cheerleaders, circa 1963.

22 Schramm had new blue jerseys designed for the Cowboys.

23 She is the director of the Dallas Cowboys Cheerleaders.

24 After losing the season opener, the Cowboys were unbeaten for 14 weeks ... unfortunately, eight of those weeks the NFL was on strike.

25 Five.

26 Philadelphia.

27 He played in it.

28 Texas Turf.

29 Mel Renfro.

30 Mel Renfro.

31 Neely signed with both the Cowboys and the Houston Oilers in 1965.

32 Ron Springs.

33 The winner of the annual Dallas-Houston pre-season game.

34 Harold Carmichael, who is 6 feet, 8 inches.

35 He caught four touchdown passes against Houston in 1970.

36 Pieces of the original Texas Stadium artificial turf.

37 Yes, the Kansas City Cowboys in the 1920s.

38 Magic.

39 Roger Staubach.

40 Tom Landry.

41 Danny White, competed with Roger Staubach for quarterback.

42 Pat Donovan and Tony Dorsett.

43 Super Bowl X, when one of the cheerleaders winked at the network cameras.

44 Six.

45 Don Meredith.

46 Mark Washington.

47 He's a scout.

48 The role of free agents in the Cowboy organization.

49 Thunder.

50 Seventeen.

51 Rushing, receiving, and on a fumble recovery.

52 Rushing, receiving, and passing (his first completion as a Cowboy was for a touchdown).

53 White has thrown for touchdowns, run for touchdowns and in 1983, he caught a touchdown pass against the Raiders.

54 As a junior against Michigan. A Navy publicist coined the phrase.

55 The Lombardi Trophy.

56 One of the original Cowboy cheerleading groups.

57 Staubach, by a year.

58 Roger Staubach and Craig Morton.

59 Steve DeBerg.

60 Preston Pearson.

61 Craig Morton and Roger Staubach.

62 No, he was with the Cowboys for 10 years, however, before being traded to San Francisco.

63 Dallas got extra draft picks after trading Craig Morton and Jack Concannon — and lost another choice by acquiring Clint Longley. Nobody said drafting was easy.

64 Nobody. They got him on waivers.

65 They had to let go of Jim Zorn, who went on to become a starter with the Seattle Seahawks.

66 Cornell Green took him to Dr. Pat Evans for a physical.

67 Blaine Nye's, in 1977.

68 Sam Baker, which goes to show that Alex Karras might have been right in describing kickers as a bit odd.

69 Yes. In 1972, he ran for 784 yards and added 390 yards in pass receptions, for a 1,174-yard total.

Was Roger Staubach more consistent? Terry Bradshaw thought he was.

70 Calvin Hill.

71 No. He finished with 5,009 yards in six years; Perkins had 6,217 in eight seasons.

72 Bill Dulin; Pettis Norman was a free agent.

73 Rolly Woolsey, Kyle Davis, and Percy Howard.

74 Billy Joe DuPree was the player. H gained the yards on a revers handoff and the kickoff return itse was charged to the other player.

75 Not exactly. He attempted seven passes in his career, completing five and having two intercepted.

76 A montage of players, Super Bowl trophies, rings, programs, Texas Stadium, and cheerleaders.

77 Robert Steele — who was picked up because Dallas had just three other wide receivers. However, Steele never caught a pass for Dallas.

78 Five — Drew Pearson was the leader from 1974-1977; Preston was the leader in 1978.

79 Three — Calvin Hill led in 1972 and '73 and Tony Hill was the leader in 1979.

80 Robert Newhouse, who was in the middle of his career, Roger Staubach, who was in his last season, and Tony Dorsett, who already was in the top 10 in just his third season.

81 Drew and Preston Pearson, Tony Hill, Tony Dorsett, Ron Springs, and Billy Joe DuPree.

82 Defensive backs Mel Renfro, Cornell Green, Cliff Harris, and Charlie Waters, and linebackers Lee Roy Jordan and Chuck Howley.

83 Three seasons. Over the same period, he rushed for more than 3,400 yards and passed for 34 — for just under 4,500 total yards.

84 Walt Kowalczyk.

85 Ten, counting playoff games.

86 Amos Marsh. The next year he had a 101-yard return.

87 Yes, although it's been tied once.

88 Frank Clarke, Billy Howton, and Dick Bielski.

89 Dan Reeves.

90 Tony Hill.

91 Jerry Rhome. LeBaron had 80-yarders in 1961 and '62, Rhome hit one in 1965 and Don Meredith joined the list in 1966.

92 Mel Renfro against San Francisco in 1965.

93 There were no turnstiles in the Cotton Bowl.

94 Amos Marsh.

95 Dan Reeves once completed a pass to a halfback, who was then tackled in the end zone for the safety.

96 Rayfield Wright and Preston Pearson were the players with the most experience in the NFL when Pugh retired.

97 He didn't; he was on the injured-reserve list.

98 Clint Longley, when he replaced an injured Roger Staubach and led the Cowboys to a come-from-behind triumph over Washington.

99 The NFL film entitled "America's Team."

100 The South African rugby player the Cowboys brought over in hopes of finding a new punter.

101 Tom Landry wants to block the linebackers' view of the offensive formation for as long as possible.

102 Hopewell High School in Alquippa, Pa.

103 The New York Giants came to Texas Stadium and spoiled the party by beating the Cowboys.

104 Allen Green and Dick Bielski.

105 Tony Hill.

106 Mike Renfro.

107 Tony Hill.

108 Larry Cole.

109 1,007.

110 No. In fact, he rushed for only 50 yards. If he hadn't made his longest run of the day (an eight-yarder) he might have missed 1,000 by a single yard.

111 None. He was injured at the end of the third quarter. For the game, he had 66 yards on 19 carries.

112 Cheerleaders choreographer Texie Waterman.

113 She designed the Cowboys Cheerleaders' costumes.

114 To make the house payments.

115 Tony Dorsett passed Don Perkins.

116 The 114 luxury Crown Suites added to Texas Stadium following the 1984 season.

117 A punt.

118 Preston Pearson.

119 L.G. Dupre.

120 Effective punt average (yardage on a punt — minus return yards).

121 Bob Lilly, Ralph Neely, and Forrest Gregg.

122 Roger Staubach, Rayfield Wright, and Lee Roy Jordan.

123 Bob Hayes ("Hell's Hole" was a Jacksonville, Fla. slum area).

124 That was the name of a restaurant in which Efren Herrera had a part interest.

125 Korea, at U.S. military bases.

126 John Wilbur.

127 1980 (immediately following the 1980 season).

128 Staubach, because Bradshaw said Roger was more consistent.

129 1978.

130 KESS.

131 John Niland.

132 St. Louis, Washington, and Philadelphia.

133 Royal blue and white.

134 Billy Howton.

135 Duane Putnam and L.G. Dupre.

136 Two players wearing the numbers 19 and 62.

137 Billy Howton.

138 Rushing, receiving, and on a kickoff return.

139 Ray Schoenke.

140 Mr. Cowboy, Bob Lilly.

141 Bob Hayes.

142 John Wilbur.

143 Ralph Neely.

144 Amos Marsh had 100-yard days twice in 1962.

145 One ruled that he belonged to Dallas — the other that he belonged to Houston.

146 Don Meredith, behind two pass blockers.

147 Don Perkins.

148 Lee Roy Jordan (with 32).

149 One, Roger Staubach.

150 Billy Lothridge (then with Atlanta), Ron Widby of the Cowboys, and Sam Baker (then with Philadelphia).

151 Tommy McDonald (fourth), Mike Ditka (tied with Howton for fifth), and Buddy Dial and Fred Dugan (tied for seventh).

152 Falstaff Brewing Corp. in 1960.

153 He passed the 10,000-yard mark in receiving.

154 The second (Robert Newhouse); the first (Bill Thomas) played just one season.

155 Punter Duane Carrell.

156 Mike Clark.

157 Third (behind Calvin Hill and Don Perkins). He was later passed by Tony Dorsett and Robert Newhouse.

158 Preston Pearson.

159 Doug Richards (brother of Golden Richards).

160 Landry had the edge on Allen, 8-7.

ACKNOWLEDGEMENTS

First and foremost, we wish to thank Carlton Stowers, whose contribution made this book a great deal easier to accomplish.

We also want to thank the Dallas Cowboys for the use of the many photographs included in the Dallas Cowboys Trivia Challenge.

The following books were used in conjunction with other materials in the research of this book:

The Heisman: A Symbol of Excellence
How to Talk Country
Pro Football at Its Best
Great Upsets of the NFL
Winline Sports Service 1982 Draft Report
Pro Football's Ten Greatest Games
Texas Women
Bear Bryant on Winning Football
Semi-Tough
The Game-Makers
North Dallas Forty
Great Running Backs #2
A Decade of Dreams
Una Decada de Suenos
Milk for Babes
Cowboys An' Indians
The Crunch
Bob Lilly: Reflections
When All the Laughter Died in Sorrow
Winning the Big One
Pro Football's 100 Greatest Players
The Dallas Cowboys Super Wives
Next Year's Champions
Staubach: First Down, Lifetime To Go
Landry . . . The Man Inside
The Courage to Believe
Cowboys' Wives' Family Fitness Guide and Nutritional Cookbook
Sports Star Tony Dorsett: From Heisman to Super Bowl in One Year
The Dallas Cowboys: Pro or Con
Bob Lilly's All-Pro Football Fundamentals
The Kicking Game
The Semi-Official Dallas Cowboys Haters' Handbook
Celebrity Turkey Trot
Hearing the Noise: My Life in the NFL
The Franchise
The Official Dallas Cowboys Bluebook (Volumes I through V)
Dallas Cowboys: The First Twenty-Five Years
The Tony Dorsett Story
Winning Strategies in Selling
Time Enough to Win
Journey to Triumph

DALLAS COWBOYS
TRIVIA CHALLENGE CONTEST

OFFICIAL RULES

1. THE PRIZES:
> **1st: $10,000** (Guaranteed)
> **2nd:** Dallas Cowboys 25th Anniversary Commemorative Bronze
> **3rd:** 2 season tickets for 1987 season
> **4th:** Leather edition of Dallas Cowboys Anniversary Book
> **5th to 15th:** .999% fine silver Commemorative Coin

2. The contest questions consist of two parts:
> a. The first part consists of the 100 multiple choice questions found in this book.
> b. The second part, the "Tie Breakers," consists of 25 fill-in questions which will be found on the back of the official answer sheet/entry form.

3. All entries must be submitted on the official entry form which is available from:
> Dallas Cowboys Trivia Challenge
> Taylor Publishing Company
> P.O. Box 597
> Dallas, Texas 75221-0597

To obtain an entry form send a self-addressed and stamped envelope to the above address. A person may enter more than once, but must enter on an official form and must follow all rules for each entry. NO PURCHASE IS NECESSARY.

4. To submit an entry, the official entry form/answer sheet must be filled in completely and returned with a processing fee of fifty cents ($.50) in the form of cash or money order. Entries sent in without the fifty cents processing fee will not be processed and the entrant will not be contacted.

5. All entries must be postmarked no later than November 30, 1986, and must be received no later than December 8, 1986. Entries are to be mailed to:
> Dallas Cowboys Trivia Challenge
> Taylor Publishing Company
> P.O. Box 597
> Dallas, Texas 75221-0597

6. The answers to the questions are stored and will remain stored in a safe at Taylor Publishing Company. However, the answers can be found in various publications on and by the Dallas Cowboys football organization.

7. The procedure for determining the "Winner" will be as follows:
> a. The person getting the most multiple choice questions correct;
> b. In the event of a tie, then the person getting the most "Tie Breaker" questions correct;
> c. In the event of a continuing tie, then the entry form with the earliest postmark

8. In the event of a dispute, the Public Relations officials of the Dallas Cowboys football organization will act as judges in resolving any issue and the decision of these officials will be considered final.

9. This contest is void where prohibited or restricted by law. All federal, state and local laws and regulations apply. Any and all taxes imposed on winners by reason of their award will be the responsibility of the winners. The correct answers will be published in the Dallas Cowboys Weekly Newspaper in the post-Super Bowl issue. For the names of all contest winners, send a stamped, self-addressed envelope to:
> Dallas Cowboys Trivia Challenge
> Taylor Publishing Company
> P.O. Box 597
> Dallas, Texas 75221-0597

10. Contest eligibility:

The contest is open to residents of the United States, eighteen (18) years of age or older EXCEPT AND EXCLUDING:

    a. Employees and their families of Taylor Publishing Company and the Dallas Cowboys Football team and organization and all of their affiliates, divisions, advertising agencies and sales representatives;

    b. The authors and their families;

    c. Past members of the Dallas Cowboys football team;

    d. Members and their families of the "media" presently covering the Dallas Cowboys football team;

All winners may be asked to sign statements confirming eligibility.

11. Additional rules/conditions:

    a. All entries will become the property of Taylor Publishing Company and will not be returned, and no processing fees will be returned.

    b. The Dallas Cowboys will not provide answers to any questions during the term of this contest. Any individual caught attempting to obtain answers from the Dallas Cowboys will be disqualified.

    c. A winner may decline his prize.

    d. Except for the first place prize, which is guaranteed, and will be paid by a certified check, prizes listed may be substituted by prizes of equal or greater value.

    e. The winners' names and likenesses may be used for publicity purposes.

    f. Copies of or subscriptions to the Dallas Cowboys Weekly may be obtained by contacting:

    Circulation Department
    Dallas Cowboys Weekly
    Cowboys Center
    1 Cowboy Parkway
    Irving, Texas 75063-4727
    (214) 556-9900

ABOUT THE AUTHORS

Gary Stratton has been with *The Dallas Morning News* for more than 11 years, the last five years as the Wire Editor. Prior to joining *The News,* he was the Sports Editor at *The Irving Daily News* (where he covered the Dallas Cowboys for more than a year) and an Assistant News Editor at *The Abilene Reporter News.* He has also worked in the sports department of *The Waco Tribune-Herald.*

Robert Krug is a writer/editor for *The Bowling News.* He previously worked for the *Fort Worth Star Telegram, The Dallas Morning News, The San Angelo Standard-Times, D/FW Metroplex High School Football Magazine, The Las Colinas Journal, The Irving Daily News,* Angelo State University and peanuts, not in any particular order.